THE TRANSCENDENTAL MEDITATION PRIMER

Patricia Drake Hemingway

THE TRANSCEN-DENTAL MEDITATION PRIMER

How to Stop Tension & Start Living

DAVID McKAY COMPANY, INC.   NEW YORK

Third Printing, October 1975

Library of Congress Cataloging in Publication Data

Hemingway, Patricia Drake.
    Stop tension and start living.

    Bibliography: p.
    Includes index.
    1. Transcendental meditation. I. Title.
BL627.H43   294   75–6918
ISBN 0–679–50554–7

Transcendental Meditation and TM® are the service marks of World Plan Executive Council—United States.

MANUFACTURED IN THE UNITED STATES OF AMERICA

Designed by Bob Antler

I dedicate this book to my grandfather,
the late Reverend Dr. George Henry Hemingway,
for lighting my way;
to Grace, who pointed out the path;
and to Helen, who had the idea and the faith in me
that I should write about it . . .

P.D.H.

ACKNOWLEDGMENTS

My grateful thanks to:

All the young people at SIMS for helping me to get this all together: Don Leopold, Michael, Rene, Harry, Ken, Bob Boyer, Bob Kory, Spencer Smith, and especially Leslie and Leonard Goldman, not only for their valued assistance but for their charming hospitality and encouragement. You have all renewed my faith in the younger generation.

Sandy Cole for the loan of her valuable and precious reference books that were of such great help to me . . .

Paul, Fritz and Charles for their steady encouragement . . .

Big Al and Little O for the unstinting use of their diggin's . . .

Greg Mowery for his willing and able assistance in

obtaining reprint permissions and a hundred other necessary things . . .

Grace Knowlton, who pointed out the path . . .

Mrs. Eleanor Rawson and Sandi Gelles-Cole, my editors, for their support and invaluable editorial assistance . . .

And last but not least, to Helen Brann and Sterling Lord, my agents, without whose terrific hope, help and talent this book would never have been.

P.D.H.

CONTENTS

LIST OF ILLUSTRATIONS

Credits for the charts used in this book can be found in the Appendix.

In most cases, the names of people mentioned herein have been changed to insure their privacy.

P.D.H.

INTRODUCTION

How to Meditate

"Meditation," for those who haven't thought about it since reading Thoreau at Walden Pond, may sound impossible for the average person with an average day to get through. That is a fallacy.

All it takes to meditate is:

1. You, in as quiet a place as you can find
2. A reasonably comfortable chair (or sit against a tree)
3. Twenty minutes of your time at the beginning of your day and twenty minutes before your evening's activities begin

Who Can Meditate

This is a book about an actual, viable way to overcome a major problem that touches each of us at some point in our lives and is responsible for as much human suffering as wars, famine and pestilence. That problem is tension. We all suffer from tension and many of us will die from it.

There are no panaceas I know of for our global problems, but there is an answer to overcoming stress and tension that is centuries old and yet only recently has been rediscovered and made available to all of us in the Western World. It is called Transcendental Meditation.

Through the application of this simple but miraculous process, any of us can immediately and actually improve our lives and start enjoying a sense of peace and fulfillment that will continue to grow throughout our existence.

This book will explain in laymen's terms what TM is and how it can and does relieve our tensions. There is no hocus-pocus abracadabra involved; no strict disciplinary regime; no complicated yoga exercises required—no special temples are needed, no choirs or congregations. It is a private experience through which all of us can gain admittance to a new world whose dimensions are infinite and beautiful.

About Maharishi Mahesh Yogi

He was born at the end of World War I in British India, the third of four children of a government-employed forest ranger of the *Kayastha* caste (sort of middle class).

He graduated from Allahabad University with a degree in physics in 1942.

In the early 1940s he met Swami Brahmananda Saraswati, the Jagadguru Bhagwan Shankaracharya or "Guru Dev" (divine teacher), who was one of the four main spiritual leaders of India.

Maharishi became a disciple of Guru Dev and studied with him for thirteen years. When Guru Dev was about to die he charged Maharishi with teaching laymen, including the Western World, a simple means to meditate. Maharishi went into seclusion in the Himalayas. When he emerged, he had developed the technique for TM.

His headquarters are presently in Switzerland. He now lives there very simply and says of material wealth, "I have no pockets." He is a lifelong celibate and vegetarian.

An Ancient Sufi Fable

Four men, a Persian, Turk, Arab and Greek were standing on a village street. These traveling companions were arguing over spending a coin that was all the money left between them.

"I want to buy angur," said the Persian.

"I want to buy uzum," said the Turk.

"I want to buy inab," said the Arab.

"No," said the Greek, "we should get stafil."

Another traveler passing by, a linguist, said, "Give me the coin. I will satisfy all your desires."

At first they would not trust him, but eventually they gave him the coin. He went to the fruit seller and bought four bunches of grapes which he gave to the four travelers.

"This is my angur," said the Persian.

"But this is what I call uzum," said the Turk.

"You have brought me inab," said the Arab.

"No," said the Greek, "in my language this is stafil."

People know that they want something because there

is an inner need existing in them. They give it different names but it is the same thing.

Idries Shah
The Sufis

BEGINNINGS

THE BEGINNING

SHORTLY before getting interested in TM I was visiting my friend Helen at her home in Connecticut. We were having dinner with Jim Lancaster, who is the head of a publishing house in Boston/New York. We were all about the same age—pushing fifty, as it's laughingly called.

Jim started it over coffee and brandy. Out of left field he said, "Helen, there is something I don't understand and it's been depressing me for some time now."

He had known Helen for many years. He was married to a college friend of hers, and although they didn't see that much of each other, it was clear their bond went back a long time. He continued, "Here I am. I've got a wonderful wife whom I love deeply and who loves me. We have two beautiful, healthy, intelligent children. I have accomplished in my business life all that I set out to do. I'm proud of my company, my authors and my integrity, and I've made enough money so that I need never worry about money again. I've really got it all, but I keep having the feeling that I'm missing something. Something big has been left out of

3

my life. What's next? Where is that new mountain to climb?"

Helen and I were both listening intently. What he had said sunk in. Practically everyone we knew, ourselves included, felt more or less the same way. What had we all done wrong? Where was the sense of fulfillment we should be feeling? And what would be our next challenge?

Again, a few weeks later I was having dinner with Helen and another friend of hers, this time her old boarding-school roommate, Faith Winston, the wife of yet another successful publisher in New York. The moment we were introduced, I sensed something about her, a lovely quality that I couldn't quite define.

She is a talented and successful sculptor, in her early forties, tall, elegant and beautiful. The more I looked and listened to her the more I began to realize her radiance was inner as well as exterior. *That* was the quality that, at first, I couldn't place.

Helen said to her, "You look wonderful, happy."

She replied, with an entrancing, shy grin, "Yes, I guess I *am* happy," as though embarrassed to admit it.

Helen persisted. "Well, are you still going to the same analyst?"

Faith replied, "Yes, but that isn't it . . ."

We began discussing the work we were all doing, the rewards and the disappointments involved. When again one of us mentioned her unusual glow of good health and good spirits (in spite of all the obvious stress of living with a high-powered, complex husband, raising four children and pursuing a career of her own), she admitted, almost embarrassed, that she had been "doing" Transcendental Meditation for over two months. Helen asked her what it was and what it had done for her. Again, she smiled shyly.

She searched for the right words for a moment before she answered.

"Well, Helen, you've known me for a long time, maybe longer than anyone. It's hard to explain, but all my life I have felt rough inside and now for the first time in my life I feel smooth inside."

It must have been at that moment that I decided I wanted to investigate whatever it was that Faith was describing. She had just expressed what I had felt about myself all my life; that I felt rough inside.

Another few days went by and due to the pressures of my daily commitments to life I did not follow through on my plan to investigate TM. While getting ready for work one morning, I was watching the "Today" show, on which Barbara Walters was interviewing a guest about TM. I called the network immediately and was told I could find out more about TM at the SIMS (Students International Meditation Society) Center in the Hotel Wentworth. When I called SIMS, I was told that the course consists of two free introductory lectures followed, if one decides to go ahead, with four consecutive two-hour sessions, the first one of private instruction.

The next time I saw Helen I said, "Listen, if you're not busy, there's an introductory lecture about Transcendental Meditation on tonight, free. What can hurt?"

We arrived at the Hotel Wentworth on West Forty-sixth Street by cab promptly at 6:30 P.M.

It reminded me of any number of Broadway hotels—that third-class look and smell that had eroded the entire Broadway area after World War II, the kind of seedy feeling in the lobby that it had seen better days.

At that hour the lobby was bustling with a cross section of its own peculiar local color—the registered guests. A glorious composite of pimps and hookers; little old ladies-in-residence living out the remainder of their lives on fixed incomes; trim, efficient airlines personnel just in from Cairo for the night; and the tourists who wanted a reasonably priced, clean hotel in the heart of town for their yearly visit to the Big Apple to see the top three Broadway shows, do a little shopping and carry the cultural word back to their friends in the hinterlands.

Helen is an even bigger snob than I am. Everything around us drew us imperceptibly closer lest we become contaminated by the air.

A sign on the stair door said "SCI [Science of Creative Intelligence]—Transcendental Meditation Center, Second Floor." We took the elevator.

We got off in a narrow corridor that had just been painted bright yellow. They had not bothered to stop at the molding. *Everything* was yellow and wet. To the right a sign said "Reception" and to the left a sign said "Lecture."

I glanced at Helen to see how she was reacting. After all, it was my idea and even *I* was beginning to have trepidations. However, she pushed ahead through the door with determination. Once Helen sets her mind to something, that's it!

A sign on the lecture room door said "Please close door quietly." The room was medium size, not yellow, thank God, but white walled, with dark woodwork. There were about forty to fifty metal folding chairs set up in neat rows with a center aisle. There were about five people in the room sitting as far apart as possible.

The first thing that struck me was the silence. Hallowed places like churches and solemn occasions like funerals always set off the giggles in me—my aunt's stomach rumbling in church was enough to send my brother and me into paroxysms of stifled laughter. My analyst, years later, decided it was indeed a form of hysteria, that I really did feel all those things like sorrow and holy respect but that I couldn't react appropriately. I stole another glance at Helen, who wasn't amused. We chose chairs in the back close to the exit. (I had just read Carlos Castañeda's *A Separate Reality* and wondered what chair *he* would have chosen, before and after the experience.)

The silence inhibited us from talking. There was a table to the right of the entrance full of literature about TM. I scooped up a handful for each of us, and as we glanced through it, more people began to filter into the room. Then, as the room was almost half filled, someone turned on the bright ceiling light and we could take a good look at our "classmates."

I believe I can speak for both Helen and myself when I say we were visibly relieved to find that we weren't sitting amidst a group of total freaks. By the time the room was full (they had to bring in more chairs), we were sitting in a room full of average New Yorkers.

There was an attractive black housewife with a cane and a broken-ankle limp sitting directly behind us. Right in front of us sat a couple in their middle thirties, well groomed and well dressed (he looked like a successful but harassed advertising executive—and it turned out he was in TV). Intuition told me that his wife had dragged him to the meeting under penalty of God knows what. He had that I-have-just-run-out-of-a-meeting-with-an-important-client-for-this-nonsense-but-anything-to-shut-you-up-*darling* look about him. There were the long- (but clean-) haired young men and women scattered about in a variety of attire— dresses, suits and ties to dungarees and sandals; the average quota of fatties, both men and women; the well-coiffed but graying well-heeled Jewish matron from Westchester; the Century Country Club type dripping in Gucci, Pucci and

Buccellati daytime gold baubles (she was alone); a middle-aged male physiologist dressed like a middle-aged male physiologist; the above-it-all menopausal redhead who wants to give the appearance that she has just come out of curiosity because *she's* perfectly happy—the only thing that gives her away is the quart-a-day face and the twitching hands; and of course the few young, scholarly-looking maiden types who, with an open mind, are out for anything that might improve their and the world's lot.

But *they* weren't why we were there. Two young people in their early twenties, the instructors, appeared at the front of the room. The boy, handsome, clean shaven, was immaculately dressed in a tan suit, hair not too long, not too short. The girl could have stepped out of a Botticelli painting. Her shining chestnut hair framed an exquisite madonna countenance. The two of them looked so pure, so good, so happy that I realized that I had forgotten that all young people used to look like that. I think it was their shining eyes that held me.

Perhaps I should interject here, if I'm going to be totally honest, that my thought processes went something like this. As I said, I was impressed with those two shining innocents standing up there before us. Then my more realistic self surfaced. I am in my late forties. I have lived in some of the world's most sophisticated towns and cities. I have been married and divorced. I have, like most of my generation, lived both too hard and too little; and I looked up at these young, inexperienced faces and thought: what in hell can they offer me or am I ready to take from them?

With poise, the instructors took command at once. The girl introduced her partner and herself to the audience as Harry and Rene. Then she asked how many people had attended the lecture because they had heard about it from a friend. Almost everyone raised their hands, including Helen and me.

Rene went on to explain that TM is *not* a religion, *not* a philosophy. It is a mental technique that provides the benefits of a very deep rest: energy, clarity, awareness. She explained that TM is a technique that enables us to refine our thoughts and give the body a deep, deep rest at the same time—a deeper rest than a good night's sleep. She went on to point out that all our activity is based on thought. And if we can tap the origin of our thoughts, we tap the origin of our creative intelligence. She compared this base, this origin of thought, to a vast reservoir that is there for the tapping if you know the technique. Being a writer, that had a ring to it for me, an appealing ring. I sneaked a look over at Helen to see how she was reacting, but her expression was stone-faced. At least she was listening.

At one point in the lecture, Rene asked us rhetorically if we had ever felt like our lives were similar to a small boat in a rocky ocean, being tossed to and fro by the wind and the waves, seemingly without any control of our destiny. I wouldn't swear to it but it seemed to me an uneasy stir occurred in many places in the room, mine and Helen's included.

Then Rene drew a simple diagram on the blackboard consisting of a lot of circles, the largest at the top and diminishing to a small dot at the bottom. She compared these circles to our thought and consciousness levels that would, through proper meditation, decrease like the circles on the blackboard. Alongside the circles she drew a grid with dots scattered through it that represented stress points and explained how the process worked. Maybe it was too simple for my quirky head, but it wasn't exactly clear to me. However, I held my tongue when the question-and-answer time came. (I was damned if I was going to expose myself as the dumb-dumb in the room.) Fortunately someone else was equally confused and asked her to repeat the explanation. Even then I still wasn't sure I understood precisely what she was getting at or how it worked. Again I kept quiet.

Someone raised his hand.

"I'm a good Christian," he said proudly, looking defiantly around the room as though he were surrounded by infidels. "Will this interfere with my religion?"

Apparently his question was not unique. Several people seemed glad that he had raised the subject. Both Rene and Harry assured him in no uncertain terms that they too understood that "the Lord thy God was a jealous God" and that TM would in no way place any other Gods before Him —that TM is compatible with all religions.

A woman in the rear either hadn't heard or didn't trust the qualification "Christian." She said, "Is it all right for Catholics?"

Everybody snickered a little except Helen and me, who wanted to "get on with it" and hear some questions and answers that might possibly relate more to us.

Then a sharply dressed young man got the floor. In a heckling tone he said, "A friend of mine went to that big bash in Houston for the young Guru Ji a short time ago. I saw my friend the next day and he swore to me that he had really seen the White Light. I mean, man, he really was *blissed out* after just seeing this kid once. I mean, like, he never stopped talking about it. What's TM got that this young guru doesn't give you in one meeting?"

For those of you who are not up to date on this highly controversial young man, Maharaj Ji, Millennium '73 was the name of the big bash held in the Houston Astrodome on November 11, 1973, sponsored by followers of this sixteen-year-old "God." He heads a group of *Premies* (an Indian word meaning "lover of God") some forty to fifty thousand strong, according to their figures. They belong to a Colorado tax-exempt foundation called The Divine Light

Chart 1

RENE EXPLAINED THE DIAGRAM BY USING MAHARISHI'S ANALOGY OF THE MIND BEING LIKE THE OCEAN. A THOUGHT STARTS FROM THE DEEPEST LEVEL OF THE OCEAN OF MIND. THE SURFACE LEVEL IS COMPARED TO THE CONSCIOUS MIND.

THOUGHTS START ON THE DEEPEST LEVEL LIKE A BUBBLE STARTS AT THE OCEAN'S BOTTOM. AS THE BUBBLE RISES IT BECOMES PROGRESSIVELY LARGER UNTIL IT SURFACES AND IS RECOGNIZED CONSCIOUSLY AS A BUBBLE (OR THOUGHT). IT RISES THROUGH THE ENTIRE DEPTH OF CONSCIOUSNESS. THE POINT BEING THAT THROUGH THE PRACTICE OF TM THE THOUGHT BUBBLE COULD BE APPRECIATED THROUGH ALL THE LEVELS OF CONSCIOUSNESS AND NOT JUST AT THE SURFACE LEVEL, THEREBY EXPANDING THE POWER OF THE CONSCIOUS MIND MANYFOLD, I.E., AS YOUR CONSCIOUSNESS TRANSCENDS ALL THE WAY TO THE BOTTOM IT HAS REACHED THE SOURCE OF ALL CREATIVE INTELLIGENCE.

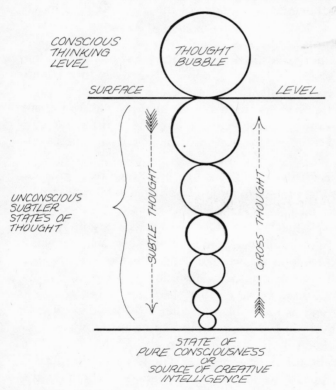

CONSCIOUS THINKING LEVEL

THOUGHT BUBBLE

SURFACE   LEVEL

UNCONSCIOUS SUBTLER STATES OF THOUGHT

SUBTLE THOUGHT

GROSS THOUGHT

STATE OF
PURE CONSCIOUSNESS
OR
SOURCE OF CREATIVE
INTELLIGENCE

AUTHOR'S NOTE: THIS IS THE AUTHOR'S VERSION OF BUBBLE CONSCIOUSNESS. NOT OFFICIAL.

Mission, which was founded by young Maharaj Ji.

According to *The New York Post,* the Mission owns fifty-six cars and trucks, and one motorcycle; of this impressive fleet, a Maserati, a Rolls Royce and three Mercedes Benzes are reserved for the personal use of Ji and his immediate family. He flies about in a privately owned jet and his mission reports an annual budget of the nice round figure of three million dollars.

The New York Times quotes a landsman of his, Swami A. C. Bhaktivedanta, founder of the Hare Krishna movement, as denouncing the baby guru as "a cheap cheat who takes advantage of fools."

Another issue of the *Times* that covered the Millennium '73 happening quotes one of his *Premies,* former antiwar activist Rennie Davis, as saying in reference to Ji, ". . . very soon every single human being will know the one who was waited for by every religion of all times has actually come . . ." (meaning Guru Ji, of course, the second Christ).

He is credited with starting one of the fastest-growing religious movements in the United States. Ji himself says his aim is to bring world peace by bringing "inner peace through spiritual knowledge." He calls himself "Perfect Master," a term that refers to his ability to teach that which is perfect, such as knowledge of God.

Although he is called by his followers "The Lord of the Universe," they also admit that "he is a little boy as well as a God," and as such "likes appliances" like Maseratis, jet planes, etc.—so followers should contribute toward these items to keep the Baby God happy!

For the privilege of seeing "The Divine White Light" (which appears to consist of a series of techniques that apparently stop the flow of blood to certain parts of the body for periods of time, making you see white light), you are supposed to commit yourself to following and contributing to his upkeep for the rest of your life.

I experienced a rather uncomfortable feeling of compassion for Harry and Rene, thinking they had been put on the spot by this smart-ass. Rene let his question sink in for a few seconds before she smiled kindly at him, as though she were dealing with a small child who has asked a grown-up a question that is sure to be a stumper and the child knows it. She said quietly, slowly, "Well, I guess the difference is, instead of being 'blissed out,' in TM you 'bliss *in.*'" A murmur of appreciation filled the room. She won that round, hands down.

By now both Helen and I were getting fidgety, and I was dying for a cigarette. But we held out a few more minutes and it was over. We were all told to come back at the same time, two nights later, *if* we were still interested. No hard sell.

INTRODUCTORY LECTURES

2

RETURN we did, after a minimum of discussion between us. Although nothing in the first lecture had done much to turn us on, by the same token, nothing had transpired to turn us off.

By now the group had thinned down to about twenty-five people. Rene was there but Harry had been replaced by a young man who had just graduated from medical school.

Rene continued her discourse, this time speaking about the physiological benefits derived from TM; she mentioned phrases like "bliss consciousness," "cosmic consciousness"; and she talked about harmony, peace, and the state of being. I didn't fully understand a lot of what she was saying but I assumed that those points would be clarified later in the course, which they were; and we will explore them later in this book.

Between the young doctor and Rene, all questions that came up were fielded with professional aptitude and undying patience. Weeks later, when this book project became a reality, I cornered the doctor and asked if he would be good enough to let me ask him some questions. He readily agreed, and here are the results.

Q. Exactly what *is* Transcendental Meditation?
A. Literally, it means transcending thought. It is also the name of a simple technique whereby we can get to the basis, the origin, of all our thought and tap its almost infinite resources. Medical science tells us that man only uses between five and ten percent of his mind's potential, of his creativeness. By practicing TM regularly over a period of time, man can realize and utilize, not only in his work life but his private life, his full potential.

Q. Is learning TM difficult? Do you ever find that there are people who cannot learn to do it or that they get discouraged because it takes them too long to see any results?
A. No, to my knowledge we've never yet lost a potential meditator because he was not able to learn the technique of meditation after his first two-hour period of personal instruction. [This happens in the first day of class after the two introductory lectures.] Of course, there have been some who "dropped out" afterward for various reasons of their own, but by and large meditators stay with it because they soon become aware of the tremendously beneficial effect it has on their daily lives. Meditation is easy, easy and natural—and so are the results.

Q. What is the "mantra"? What is its purpose?
A. The mantra is a word that is given to each person by his instructor the first day he is initiated into meditation. Instead of a word, it is more accurately described as a sound. The word "mantra" is derived from Sanskrit and, loosely translated, means "the sound whose effects are

known." Scholars of meditation say that each individual differs in the quality of the sounds that are most soothing to his individual personality and physical type. The right selection of a mantra for a particular individual is of vital importance. Therefore, the instructor has been taught to take into account certain aspects of each individual before assigning him or her a mantra. The mantra is assigned in the first private session. Then the meditator is taught to use this mantra as a device with which to meditate properly so that he can receive the fullest benefits, the deepest rest, from the meditation.

After meditating a short time, the mantra becomes a part of you. What starts out as a meaningless foreign-sounding word to you in the beginning becomes a soothing vibration or tone inside of you that helps you to achieve deep meditation.

Q. Why is the meditator told to keep the mantra secret?

A. As for keeping your mantra a secret, the reasons are twofold. The first being oneself. After a brief period of meditating, this mantra, if brought to the surface and exposed to the efforts of the lip and tongue to pronounce it to another person . . . [He hesitated, then clarified.] I can only liken it to a seedling that has begun to grow. You can see the growth above the soil, but not the progress of its roots. If you were to pull up the delicate seedling to see how the roots were growing you would find it almost impossible to replace it exactly again without damaging or retarding or even killing its growth. So it is with your mantra. To paraphrase an old joke, it loses something in the translation from mind to tongue.

The second reason is that the person to whom you give your mantra is undoubtedly a different kind of person than you. Consequently it wouldn't achieve the desired results and might have a deterrent effect on that person.

Our teachers have spent much time and advanced study to be able to assign the proper mantra to the right person. It is not random choice.

Q. How does one meditate?

A. It is very simple. Ideally, the meditator should have a quiet place to sit, by himself or herself, without telephones ringing, children screaming, or dogs barking. He sits in a comfortable position, preferably with head not supported. You give yourself a few moments with your eyes closed to get peacefully settled and then you begin to think the mantra—to clear the mind of thought and allow your consciousness to descend slowly. Extraneous thoughts may come into your consciousness, for instance, problems of the day that are unresolved, when you first try to meditate. Don't worry about that. Your mantra will come back to you easily and without effort. Other times you may experience a mixture of mantra and thought; sometimes you will experience an absence of thought, a mental void, which is the ideal meditation. It is truly "transcending." However, it does not matter if you don't reach that base or void every time, because it has been shown by many tests that even if it seems that your mind has been busy, even agitated with pent-up emotions, etc., mixed with thought and/or your mantra, you *still* receive the benefits of the deep rest.

You meditate for twenty minutes in the morning before you start your day's efforts and twenty minutes again in the early evening before your evening activity begins. These two sessions of rest will provide you with renewed energy, prepare you for the activity ahead.

There will be times when the conditions of meditation won't be ideal. But then do the best you can, either take ten minutes in the taxi or the commuter train or wherever. Less than ten minutes has proven to be ineffective.

Q. If one started to practice TM now, how long would it take to notice any benefits, and are these benefits concrete or abstract?

A. Well, I'll answer that in three parts.

First, as a practitioner of TM for over five years, I can attest to the benefits to myself, but they are of a personal nature that is private to each person.

Second, as a practitioner and instructor I can say without qualification or reservation that the results are immediate; from the moment you start to practice the technique of TM your body experiences a deep, deep rest. For the normal, healthy human being this produces more physical and mental energy, more clarity and originality of thought, and more productiveness. This is why management has become interested in TM for their executives. The executive who meditates seems to function better on all levels, not only on a business level, but a personal level. When he gets home at night, TM seems to enable him to throw off the day's stresses and tensions . . . to approach his family or friends as a refreshed person, who has the ability, energy and love left in him or her to enjoy those hours remaining at the end of the work day. He finds he doesn't need those two double martinis to last the evening with some semblance of civility and love.

In essence, TM is a means, a preparation for the other activities of your life. It is not a way of life but a beneficial addition for a more productive and more fulfilling life.

Third, as a medical man, I can say unqualifiedly that the benefits are immediate and cumulative. First and foremost, it gives you a deep rest. A team of Harvard researchers has concluded that even after ten minutes of TM the decrease in oxygen consumption was seventeen percent deeper than six or seven hours of sleep, a reduction of three beats per minute or a cardiac output drop of twenty-five percent, a significant reduction on the workload of the heart. For cardiac patients this could mean the difference between life or death. According to the results of other studies there is a change in "skin resistance." During stress or anxiety there is a decrease in skin resistance; while meditating, skin resistance increases, thereby significantly reducing anxiety and stress. The metabolic level shows a marked decrease during meditation indicating a state of deep body rest. The level of lactate in the blood decreases tremendously during meditation. Lactate is known as one of the causes of high blood pressure, anxiety neurosis and anxiety attacks. I have found in my own personal dealing with patients that those who practice meditation seem to heal much more rapidly. It may sound astonishing, but I would say at least three times faster.

In our TM research we have witnessed a marked decrease in drug addiction, alcoholism and even smoking. In these areas sometimes the results are visible almost immediately and sometimes it takes months, depending upon the individual, of course. But the evidence is incontrovertible. Major research in every level of medicine and rehabilitation and education is being carried on now by many universities, institutes and governments all over the world on the effects of TM on drug abuse, the stress-related illnesses, ulcers, high blood pressure, cardiac conditions, mental illnesses, bad backs, etc.

Q. Many psychoanalysts affiliated with the Freudian or Karen Horney schools show some resistance to TM. Why?
A. Many people, not only analysts, misunderstand TM. It is not, I repeat *not*, a substitute for anything, including

psychoanalysis, religion, medical advice and treatment, sleep, A.A., or anything else. It is an addition to any and/or all of the areas of your life.

Q. Is it true that there are almost six hundred thousand Americans practicing TM in the United States today, not counting the rest of the world, and that this number is doubling at least every year?

A. At least. Those figures are conservative. We hope to have at least ten percent of the population practicing TM and the Science of Creative Intelligence.

Helen and I both signed up, after assuring ourselves that the initial price of the course ($125 as this goes to press) was all we would ever have to pay. That was the one question I stuck my neck out to ask. And if I hadn't, I'm sure there were plenty of people there who would have. We were also assured that after taking the four-session course we would know how to meditate and would never have to return except for a free checkup to make sure we were doing it properly.

We made our appointments for our personal instruction for the following Monday. The only restrictions were that we were not to have smoked grass or been on any drugs other than what one's doctor prescribed for at least fifteen days. (Some joker asked about boozing it up and was patiently told it would be advisable not to arrive drunk.)

Out of curiosity I checked with the SCI and was told that the reason it is all right to drink in this quarantine period but not to smoke grass is that the physiological effect has been found to be quite different. It has been found that aspirin can be detected in the bloodstream two weeks after one has taken it (not that aspirin is necessarily bad for one), and it has also been found that meditators who smoke pot have been affected over a longer period of time from the effects of marijuana at the subtle levels of thought, particularly in the initial meditation period. The continuing effect of alcohol in the bloodstream has not been observed nor has it been observed that it affects the subtler levels of thought over a long period of time (obviously this pertains to drinking in moderation).

INITIATION

I WAS intrigued from the start because, when I signed up for the course, I was told to bring with me to the next session (which was to be my private instruction class—what the TM people call initiation) a clean white handkerchief, three different pieces of fresh fruit, and a small bunch of fresh flowers. Since I had already given them my money I didn't bother to ask why at that time.

The important day arrived. I, who with my postnasal drip should have invested in the Kleenex company years ago, since I use it by the carload, searched high and low and could not find even a clean *blue* hankie, so I went to Whelan's drugstore and bought one of those cellophane-wrapped men's handkerchiefs, stopped at a corner florist shop and spent a whole dollar forty-nine for a bunch of posies, and dropped by my local grocer to pick out the prettiest apple, pear and plum that I could find. Having dutifully assembled my kit, I grabbed a taxi to the Wentworth for my appointment.

Rene was waiting there to greet me. She asked me to

remove my shoes, bring my flowers, hankie and fruit, and follow her.

She led me to a softly lighted room furnished with two overstuffed chairs and a long table that was situated against the wall. She placed my flowers and fruit under a picture of an old Indian sage who, I was informed, was Maharishi's teacher (or guru) in India, "Guru Dev." She explained that the fruit and flower offering was simply a gesture of thanks or "an apple for the teacher." Then she said a few Indian words of thanks to the old guru and did a simple ceremony with the hankie and returned it to me. Then we got down to business.

She questioned me about my personal life (nothing too personal), my occupation, age, etc. She also had a sheet I had filled out at the first introductory lecture that enumerated any problems I might have, such as headaches, insomnia, feelings of hostility or whatever. Then she "gave" me my mantra. That is, she assigned me a mantra and repeated it to me three or four times and had me say it aloud to her to make sure I got it properly. Then she showed me how to meditate.

We meditated together for twenty minutes or so to make sure that I was doing *that* right, and that was it. Rene reminded me that I was to come back the next three evenings for three more orientation lectures.

As I left she cautioned me that my mantra should be kept secret because that was important—it was mine alone and chosen just for me. Then she said, "That's all there is to it. Now you can do it yourself."

I felt like a kid with a new toy. I couldn't wait for the next morning to try it alone—to test my wings on a solo flight into my own interior.

I got up, as usual, around eight o'clock.

The TM people had said not to eat breakfast first because the body is working when it is digesting food and not resting. But morning coffee was permissible. Having completed my usual ablutions, I set about to find the "right" place to sit. They said lying back in bed was no good because people fell asleep; besides, my cleaning lady was in the bedroom. I no sooner settled down before the dogs (three yappers) started barking at the garbage collector outside the kitchen door.

I moved to the living room and settled in again. About two seconds later the mailman started leaning on the doorbell and the phone rang simultaneously. Finally some sort of peace reigned and I managed to get through my experience with no further interruptions. (I must confess, the evening before, on my way home from the center, I was so terrified I would forget my mantra that I wrote it down phonetically in my daily diary. My instructor had had me repeat it several times to make sure I had it right, but with my feeble memory I wasn't taking any chances. Later on I was to learn that a meditator should *never* write down his or her mantra—that committing the sound to paper can distort it. However, at this writing, I've yet to meet a meditator who hasn't scribbled down the mantra and tucked it away somewhere.)

Anyway, I still had three more sessions to attend to ask any questions that might be bothering me, and even if I did forget my mantra I was sure Rene would refresh my memory, but it would have been too embarrassing to have to admit I wasn't able to remember just that one word or sound or whatever they called it. However, the mantra presented no problem. It came to me easily, without effort.

What did trouble me though were the myriad thoughts that kept running through my brain. The goal, as I understood it, is to free the mind from thought, and the mantra is to help you to do that if you get hung up on a specific train of thought to divest the mind—to give it a gentle, harmless focus. I was truly astonished at the swiftness and diversity of messages that can scurry through one's cranium in the short span of twenty minutes. (Still am.)

Afterward, being rather curious and, I like to think, scientifically objective, I began to examine what I had just experienced. Toward the last part of the twenty minutes there were, it seemed, split seconds when my mind was actually free from both extraneous thoughts and the mantra, but those moments were fleeting. Although I was aware of sounds and activity in my surroundings they were distant and unobtrusive. I was also aware that my breathing had become quite shallow. Otherwise, nothing untoward was apparent.

As well as I knew Helen, we were both strangely reticent about discussing our individual meditation with each other. At least at first. Then, toward the end of the first session following initiation, it became clear that everyone had more or less the same interferences to contend with: dogs, kids, telephones, doorbells, husbands, lovers, extraneous thoughts and problems flooding their brains. We all had had the same difficulties trying to work out our life schedules to enable us to sneak in twenty minutes twice a day. At that time if anyone had told me—told me?—*bet* me a million dollars that my life was so structured that I would find it difficult, sometimes almost impossible, to set aside those two twenty-minute periods out of my average day, I would have bet them a thousand dollars that it would be perfectly easy to do. I was dead wrong. I don't care what your occupation or non-occupation is, it is damned hard unless you are a total recluse and don't own a television set. But it *can* be done. Oh, I've missed either a morning session or an afternoon one sometimes. And some days I can manage only ten or fifteen minutes while getting somewhere in a taxi, but like the instructor said, "Your ears won't fall off if you goof once in a while any more than if you miss your full night's sleep."

That first session was extremely helpful in dispelling any doubts or fears we all had about meditation. Our instructors answered all kinds of crazy questions and by the end of the two hours we were all confident that we were bona fide meditators!

By the way, the group of people that one confronts the very first night in the introductory lecture (that is, those who return the second night) all progress at the same rate, as many of the group as possible go through initiation on the same day, and all "graduate" the same day—after the final three orientation sessions.

Most of the second session was taken up with questions from the newly initiated dealing with various physical manifestations experienced while meditating. The village idiot of our group asked in a fearful voice what would happen if he ran over the time and meditated for twenty-five minutes instead of twenty and should he count the thirty seconds or so it takes to quiet down before starting to meditate into the twenty minutes.

The instructor smiled patiently and assured him he would survive if he ran over or under his twenty minutes. He heaved a sigh of relief. We all giggled.

The physiologist asked if it was all right to scratch an itchy spot during meditation or would he have to start all over again. He was given the OK to scratch his itch without being compelled to start over. We *all* heaved a sigh of relief.

Another man complained of slight muscle spasms during meditation. He was told that they were definite signs that stress was leaving his body and that eventually, if he meditated regularly, they would diminish and disappear.

The black housewife with the cane who was the mother of three children raised her hand. Her problem was that she didn't want her family to know that she was doing TM and the only way she could steal the time in peace was to lock herself in the bathroom, but that was proving difficult since they only had one bathroom and invariably one of the kids would have to "go." More laughter. Everyone in the class tried to help her solve that dilemma but I'm not sure we did.

The following evening, the third session brought forth some rather different problems.

The harassed young ad executive whom I surmised had been talked into this thing by his wife complained that he was losing a half-hour's sleep by having to get up earlier to meditate. After ascertaining that he was a commuter, his difficulty was eliminated. He could meditate on the train. His wife gave him an I-told-you-so nudge in the ribs and smiled ever so righteously. He looked like he wanted to give her a nudge somewhere else.

Then a rather straitlaced-looking woman in her late twenties or early thirties said, in such a way that you *knew* she was talking about herself, "I have this friend who smokes marijuana. . . ." The whole room broke up in laughter. She colored a deep crimson but continued, "Will that interfere with her meditating?"

The instructor came to her rescue. "I'm glad you brought that up. We have found that most people who are into drugs of any sort gradually stop because they find that it eventually brings them down and interferes with the benefits they get from meditating."

The redhead with the quart-a-day face and twitchy hands said angrily, "I've never had trouble sleeping before in my life and now, since I've started meditating, I find I'm waking up in the middle of the night and can't get back to sleep. . . ."

The instructor looked puzzled for a moment, then she asked, "What time do you do your evening meditation?"

With her conscience clear, the redhead replied, "After the eleven-o'clock news." Again we all broke up. The instructor explained again to us all that we should meditate *before* the evening begins, not after. No wonder she couldn't get back to sleep. The energy flow derived from meditating was hitting her in the middle of the night.

A man sitting in the front complained that he fell sound asleep two different times doing his meditation. It turned out that he came home after work and lay down on his bed as he usually did for his nap before dinner. He was told not to lie down but sit upright in a straightback chair. He nodded. That made sense.

The well-heeled Jewish matron who, up to this time, had not said anything in any of the sessions spoke up and said that her husband seemed to resent the twenty minutes she took out of *his* "martini time." She was told to get in her meditation *before* he got home from work and that, eventually, when he saw how much calmer and happier she was, he would undoubtedly change his opinion about it. *That* made sense.

By the time the final session rolled around most of the logistical difficulties of the various people had been ironed out but questions concerning the mantra arose.

A nondescript little gray-haired man whom I had not noticed before spoke up. "About the mantra, just this morning I had a strange experience that almost knocked the top of my head off. . . ." More laughter. "I couldn't remember the mantra. I mean I had difficulty remembering the mantra. I'll tell you what that experience was. I heard a small thin voice say to me, 'It's a pretty good sound' and immediately the mantra came to me and I believed in the mantra. Before that I didn't believe in the mantra. It bothered me."

When the laughter died down the instructor told us that we don't have to *believe* in the mantra, we just use it, and the more we use it, the more natural and a part of us it becomes. He reiterated that the mantra is just a sound we use to clear the mind of other thought. It is a vehicle to use, *not* believe in.

The fat fellow who had been sitting across from me brought up the fact that several of his friends, when they found out he was taking the course, asked him to give them a mantra so that they could meditate without taking the course. That made me sit up and listen because some of my cheap and/or lazy friends had suggested the same thing to me. The teacher's answer was, "There are different mantras given to different people. For example, heads of industry get different mantras than housewives and mystics. 'Om,' for instance, is a mantra for mystics. Just tell your friends that if they get the wrong mantra they might wind up quitting their jobs and heading for the nearest mountain top forever—that should stop them from bugging you about it."

On that note of levity the final session was ended. Then each of us had a few minutes' private meeting with our initiator in a separate room to make sure we were thinking our mantra correctly and a final chance to ask any questions of a personal nature that might be bothering us. We were also reminded that we should come for a free-of-charge checkup once a month for the first year if we wanted to be absolutely sure that we were meditating properly.

To be perfectly honest, I walked out of that dingy hotel that night feeling as though I had really taken a giant step, and, to paraphrase Shakespeare, looking forward to greater things on heaven and earth, Patricia, than I ever dreamed could be on *my* horizons.

For the next several days I noticed some strange things happening to me during my meditation; the first was that my eyelids started to twitch as though I had developed a tic of some sort. After a few days that went away but was replaced by a ringing in my ears.

I had occasion to call Helen on the phone about something else, and during the course of our conversation she asked how my meditating was coming along.

I said, "Fine, but are you experiencing any odd things while you are meditating?"

She laughed and said, "Now that you mention it, every now and then the muscles in the back of my neck seem to jerk . . . just the tiniest bit but enough to make me aware of it. Why, what's happening to you?"

I said, "Well, at first my eyelids twitched but that went away and then my ears started to ring a lot when I was meditating."

She giggled. "How do you know your ears don't always ring and you're never quiet long enough to hear them?"

"Very amusing, Helen," I responded. "Nevertheless, I'm going to ask about it when I go for my checkup and you should too."

Sure enough, when we inquired of the checker a week or so later he told us that our symptoms were quite normal. He said most people have these manifestations of stress leaving the body during meditation. He said some people have so much stress in them that they even get migraine headaches for a while, but not to worry, everything goes away in a short time. We were both relieved to find out that we were meditating correctly and our "odd" symptoms were perfectly normal signs of de-stressing, which was one of the reasons we started TM in the first place. If ever two middle-aged career girls needed de-stressing, it was Helen and me! And I suppose, if the truth be known, having a bit of Scots in me, I was secretly delighted to have proof positive I was getting my money's worth.

THE ADVANCED LECTURES

4

Just before they showed a videotape of Maharishi, we meditated for ten minutes. The instant stillness that occurs in the small roomful of people never ceases to fascinate me. No scuffling, no coughing, no movement, not even the normal sound of breathing from the person next to you. Even if you weren't a meditator I think you would get a contact high just from the sound of silence for that brief period. It is quite phenomenal. I can only compare it to the feeling that comes over an entire theater audience when the final curtain has come down on an extraordinarily beautiful and moving stage performance—that fleeting, stunned hush before the applause begins, when there literally is not a sound to be heard. The more I think about it, both experiential feelings seem to be enhanced by constructive, communal effort, like the synergism of a magnificent choir in perfect harmony.

It was at about this stage of the game that I decided to write a book about TM and wanted to find out all I could. On the bulletin board at the Wentworth I had seen notices about advanced lectures being given (for free) on TM and the Science of Creative Intelligence and made up my mind to go. Although these lectures are not mandatory for the practice of TM, I think that, even if I hadn't decided to do the book, my natural curiosity would have led me to attend at least one of these lectures and, like I said, they were free.

My first advanced lecture was held on the second floor of the Hotel Wentworth in the same meeting room where the other lectures were held.

The instructor was a young man with horn-rimmed glasses, a thin, intellectual-looking type. The room was about one-third filled with people from many walks of life in various attire, from business clothes to dungarees.

The instructor asked first if anyone was having any trouble meditating and, if so, to please ask questions.

A gray-haired, nice-looking older gentleman spoke up and said that he had been "checked" and had been told he was meditating properly but he didn't feel that he was experiencing any change in his day-to-day life. He was certain that he was reaching the "pure consciousness level," as the instructors at TM call it, but afterward he couldn't see the purpose of it. (It's difficult to explain the concept of "pure consciousness" at this stage of the book without sounding too "fruity," but, briefly, compare your mind with a blank sheet of paper—either one that has never been written upon or one that has had everything erased and is now ready to receive a new inscription, i.e., a clear field; ganzfeld, as Dr. Robert Ornstein calls it. It is very difficult for some people to understand the value of the vacuum, the void, the nothingness. Perhaps if I use the old expression "wipe the slate clean," it would be more meaningful.)

He then said, "Let me restate my problem." Everyone laughed, not at him but for him. He smiled and said, "It's just simply that sometimes I find myself sitting there meditating and I'm disgruntled. I think to myself, "Jesus, am I sitting here with my eyes closed, squinting, because some dude over in India says I should? I'm looking or searching . . . see, I have been meditating regularly since January. I haven't missed once. . . ." He paused a second and then confessed, "Well, just once. . . ." Again, everyone guffawed, because no one hasn't missed at one time or another, and I guess they all have felt as guilty as I have when I miss—as though I have done something offensive to my body or my emotional structure. He continued, "The fact of the matter is I'm searching, I'm a neophyte too in TM, and if there are people who know I'd like to hear about it."

Another man spoke up. "Maybe I can help. I think I know what's troubling him. . . ."

There was something in the tone and quality of the second man's voice that made us all sit up and look around at him. He was dressed in a good-looking, gray-tweed sports coat and gray flannels; he was a balding man in his late fifties or early sixties, small in stature and very virile-looking. The instructor nodded for him to continue.

"Well, let's say that this gentleman would like to relate his experience to science. Let's say he has a computerized brain, and if he doesn't tune in on this computerized brain and he relaxes his brain for a given moment and doesn't associate it with anything else and the input is nil, then he will experience this blank area. And this blank area is like pure consciousness. I have a feeling that each of us associate a certain experience that we have, and some of us just can't associate the abstract and the ephemeral experience with . . . it has to be concretized. The fact is, though, that pure consciousness by its very nature is extremely abstract. You can't grab it and hold on to it. You can apprehend an experience and I think you can explain most experiences.

But this experience is different. If you want to communicate it, you can't. You can own it but you can't give it away. . . ."

I was damned impressed with his explanation of the state of "pure consciousness," or "no visible or tangible input," as he termed it, and so was the rest of the room, including the young teacher. So much so that he said, "You should be a teacher of TM."

The eloquent gentleman settled back, looking pleased with himself. The man with the question still looked a little puzzled but let it drop.

Still others complained good-naturedly about the difficulty they were encountering in setting aside their twenty minutes twice a day. My sympathies were with them. It isn't easy for some of us.

Then it was tape time. For some reason or other, TM's teacher-training courses do not seem to include a course in sound engineering. Inevitably there is always some difficulty in getting it together. Either they can't find the tape or the switch or the cord, or they have the wrong machine, or something, but eventually they proceed, usually with the help of someone in the audience more familiar than they are with fancy sound equipment. At last they get it working, and everyone settles back to view and listen to Maharishi Mahesh Yogi's lecture in living color on a twenty-one-inch TV screen.

Each of the series of lectures has a separate theme. The instructor explains the theory behind the theme. In the ones I attended, they played a videotape of Maharishi and his views on that theme. Then the theme was thrown open for questions and discussion. Among these themes was a discussion of cosmic consciousness, which is an extremely important concept to grasp for the meditator and one which I'll tell about in detail in the Creativity chapter.

Each lecture session was different. They were either extremely interesting with lively discussions or not too stimulating, depending upon the instructor and the group involved. Some of them were quite amusing and informative. My mother used to judge whether a musical was good or bad by whether or not she could walk away humming the hit tune from the show. I enjoyed these advanced lectures because I invariably walked away with some phrase or idea that made me think about it afterward. Some I can remember are: Angry words pollute the atmosphere. Do not go about lost in your own taste. Awareness is wholeness. Ignorance limits. Simple phrases, and yet not so simple once you begin to delve into them in depth. Some are original, some are not; but what's the difference if they set you thinking along constructive lines?

I found them all worthwhile in some respect. And even though some of the instructors lacked verve and perspicacity, the videotapes of their teacher made the time spent worthwhile. As usual, it is the teacher who makes the course interesting, not the course that makes the teacher interesting.

The more meetings and lectures I attended, the more I realized how fortunate we were to have had such good instructors in Rene and Harry and Michael (the young doctor), whose innate charm and intelligence infected their classes and transmitted their enthusiasm to their audiences. However, just like in school, some teachers were better than others. Many of the young instructors of TM are rather lackluster. That is one of the few criticisms I have run across in the TM movement, the quality of the instructors. This is not only my observation but the complaint of many intelligent people who, for this reason, have not continued beyond the first or second advanced lecture. They say the teachers teach by rote; they answer questions by rote, like

Bell Telephone operators are taught to do. The TM movement says that this is because Maharishi doesn't want his
teaching watered down by each teacher expressing himself
in a different way and thus each changing the meaning a
little bit.

Maharishi might explain his insistence on having all his
instructors be strict conformists by using the following parable:

> A distant kinsman on a visit brought Nasrudin a duck for
> a gift. Nasrudin was pleased. He had the bird cooked and
> served to his guest for dinner that night. Shortly thereafter
> one visitor after another started to call, each the friend of the
> friend of the man who brought the duck. The friends, how-
> ever, arrived empty handed. After several of these visits
> Nasrudin became annoyed. Then one day another stranger
> appeared with an offering. "I am the friend of the friend of
> the kinsman who brought you the duck." He sat down like
> all the rest expecting a meal. Nasrudin presented him with
> a bowl of hot water. "What is this?" Nasrudin replied, "That
> is the soup of the soup of the soup of the duck which was
> brought by my kinsman."

This is what the TM people are afraid will happen to
Maharishi's teaching. He contends that the path to knowledge has existed for centuries but became lost through
progressively weakened, watered down teaching of the
doctrine.

The teacher, the leader, is Maharishi Mahesh Yogi. He
is almost indescribable. I mean you have to see him and
hear him to know what I am talking about. My first impression from the videotape was of a small, funny-looking little
man sitting cross-legged, lotus position, in a simple white
robe, fondling a single long-stemmed rose, using it almost
as a baton to lovingly orchestrate his conversational points.

His long gray hair falls abundantly about a face that has a very pixielike quality because of the rather devilish twinkle in his wide-set, kindly eyes. When I first heard his voice, although he was speaking articulate, perfect English, it was difficult for me to understand him. It, too, was pixielike with its East Indian tonal phrasing, and yet it was also many textured, ranging from high-pitched lilt to an almost sensual resonance. It wasn't until I had heard about three tapes that my ears became accustomed enough to fully encompass the rhythm of his speech—then it became a beautiful sound. Only then could I comprehend what he was saying. His rhetoric is delightful, punctuated with wry wit, a touch of irony, humor and profound wisdom. He is a rare combination of poet, sage and statesman as he eloquently propounds his theories, hopes and dreams for the world's future employment of the techniques of TM and the Science of Creative Intelligence. It would be a world where man could channel his aggressiveness and energy for the true fulfillment and betterment of himself and hence the rest of mankind.

He did not leave his mountaintop in the Himalayas to induce Western men to become Eastern mystics or to lead just the contemplative life, but to teach them to live in their world in harmony and peace and to comprehend and enjoy the abundance of nature and the natural processes. Maharishi impressed me as a noble man with a noble goal.

Here is a list of the themes from some of the advanced lectures:

Consciousness and Existence
Knowledge Is Structured in Consciousness
Styles of Functioning of the Nervous System—States of
    Consciousness
Range of Life and Creative Intelligence

Thought and Feeling
Expanding Values of Love and Refinement of Perception—Growth from the State of Full Awareness
Desire, Action and Fulfillment
Right and Wrong Action—Basis of Fundamental Values of Life-Supporting Action
Growth and Force of Evolution
Nature of Loss and Revival of Knowledge
Role of Activity in Growth of Consciousness
Supreme Knowledge—Ultimate Value of Perception
Ignorance and Self-Realization
Basis of All Problems—Localized Awareness vs. Unbounded Awareness
Objective and Subjective Bases of Gaining Knowledge
TM and the Fulfillment of Religion
Suffering—Origin and Elimination
TM and the Philosophy of Yoga

Don't let some of the titles frighten you off. They are explained and made interesting and applicable in our everyday lives. No great IQ is required to understand them. Just the time and desire. (Once again, there is no additional charge for attending these lectures at the centers.)

ON YOUR MARK, GET SET . . . GO!

ENERGY AND STRESS

5

To be in the world but not of it, free from
ambition, greed, intellectual pride, blind
obedience to a custom, or awe of persons higher
in rank—that is the Sufis ideal.

THE SUFIS

MOST of us fall far short of our "ideal." God knows, life
is not easy at best. Sometimes just to survive takes all
our strength and resources. There are very few of us who
can sit on top of the mountain in the Himalayas, impervious
to wind, rain, cold and hunger, and lead a totally contemplative existence. Most of us must work, raise families, provide them with warmth and shelter, food and love, even
if it kills us, which it sometimes does—and then they
are without us. All the life insurance in the world cannot replace your tender, loving care when you are
gone. The world is full of bereft, lonely widows, wid-
owers and children who cannot replace *you*. The old
grim reaper is no respecter of nationality, creed, financial status or anything else. It is up to *you* to stay alive.

But who wants *just* to stay alive . . . just to exist?

Our lives should not be *just* worry and woe and toil and trouble. Our lives should have purpose, meaning, joy, love and fulfillment. The former seem to be bestowed on us daily, either by our own bad management or sometimes just force of circumstances. But the latter we must strive for, *make* them happen. What stops us? We are so worried about tomorrows that we can't enjoy our todays. And each worry and woe and trouble builds tension and stress.

Maharishi says that man has the right and the capability to live a fulfilled life. It is his choice to take advantage of that opportunity or ignore it and his degree of happiness will follow accordingly.

I was reading somewhere recently that no mother wakes up in the morning *wanting* to scream at her children. But invariably children do things they shouldn't and mothers eventually scream when their nerves can't stand another moment of it all. Then the stress spreads to the children and the mother feels guilty. Then the old man comes home from *his* lovely day at the office where things haven't been exactly perfection. He lost a big account, his boss was looking strangely at him, and his priceless secretary (who has covered for him totally for five years) announced that she's getting married and giving him a month's notice. On his way home he's so upset he screams at the taxi driver for no good reason, and the driver in turn gets angry and screams at *his* wife and kids. And the music goes round and round. Where does it all end? How?

Each person in that cycle would have the power to stop the momentum if he didn't react the way he did, defensively. A basic difference between wild animals and domesticated animals is that if a door slams on your dog's tail he doesn't turn around and rip *you* to death, but a wild animal would blame you instinctively for what happened under the same circumstances. We were all brought up in a so-called Christian world, and the Christian ethic is to "turn the other cheek." Do you turn the other cheek when you are unjustly attacked? Do you feel *sorry* for the man who wronged you or do you strike back in verbal indignation? Maybe not if he's bigger than you are. Maybe then you just go around the rest of the day nurturing your injured pride and taking it out on someone smaller in size and stature than you. Or maybe you're the kind of person who keeps it inside smoldering and building up stress. If you do take it out on someone else unjustly, you probably feel guilty. Guilt builds stress. Anger builds stress. Hate builds stress. Rejection builds stress. Frustration builds stress. If we want to live in today's hectic world as functioning, wheeling-dealing members of a complicated, ever-changing society, we either have to adapt or perish. Many of us perish long before our time because we cannot adapt to or eliminate the daily stresses that we encounter and accumulate.

The first time I ever related stress to myself was when I went to a new dentist (the last two had died out from under me). I was forty-one, a few long years ago. He examined my mouth, read the X rays, shook his head and said, "Well, your teeth are all right, your gums are fine, but I'm afraid the bones are gone. With a series of treatments from a good periodontist you may, with any luck, keep your teeth for another five years."

It seemed to me I had spent a good part of my life (not to mention agony and money) in dentists' chairs and knew that I had taken more than average care of my teeth. I told him as much and angrily said that obviously dentists were charlatans of the first degree—otherwise how could it have happened?

He laughed good-naturedly and said, "No, I'm afraid it's due to stress. That's a major factor in bone deterioration." For another thousand dollars the periodontist agreed with him. He even went further. *He* said "Stress is a killer."

"Stress," I thought. To me stress meant "to stress a point" or maybe in construction terms, "the stress points of a bridge," but stress as a killer? That was a new twist!

Being an avid reader of *The New York Times* obit page (not just for morbid curiosity but also to keep my address book current), I had been aware for some time that an awful lot of people, mostly men, were knocking off at what should have been their prime of life, between their forties and late fifties. Now these gentlemen weren't potter's field types; they were successful, recognized men of property and standing in the community (otherwise they wouldn't be in the *Times*'s obit page). Ever since my visit to the dentists I had searched in vain for *stress* to be listed as the cause of death. I asked my own physician if she had ever seen it on a death certificate. "Never," she replied, looking oddly at me.

Even if you think you have a happy, peaceful life, stress builds up. A very happy, peaceful young friend of mine had her phone go out of order a few years ago. She has a young son and doesn't work. Her days are spent gossiping on the phone to her friends. She went to the corner pay phone and reported it to the New York Telephone Company. They promised to be there the next day between nine and five, which meant she had to stay home to let the repairman in. The next day came and went, no repairman. Again she went to the corner pay phone. Again the phone company promised faithfully they would be there the following day between nine and five. Again she was a prisoner—a prisoner without a phone. This went on for twenty-eight days at the end of which she was just about ready for the funny farm, literally a nervous wreck. For her a telephone was a vital organ. For others it may be the dishwasher that takes days to get repaired. Unless we live on mountain tops in seclusion without what we consider the necessities of life, we have to cope with stressful situations because nothing runs smoothly anymore. Every day we turn around there is some sort of strike or another with which we must deal as best we can.

All these things deplete our energy and increase tension. I make a distinction between pressure and stress. Some people work well under "pressure." It gives them the needed stimulus, the kick in the backside, to get moving, but stress bogs you down like quicksand. The more stress that builds up in us the less able we are to cope. Finally even the simplest problems become insurmountable dilemmas. Our priorities become confused and our options lost in the confusion; it is a vicious circle that ultimately sucks us down into a quagmire, draining us both mentally and physically of our limited energies.

We all need all the energy we can muster to live a joyful existence; we need the energy to apply ourselves to the fruitful pursuits of life that replenish and even add to our energy supply. We need natural energy, not the false energy that momentarily comes from the blast of your first double Scotch but which later debilitates and depresses you and makes you more tired than you were before. We should think of our energy supply as we think of our money. If we want it to grow we have to place it where it bears the most interest with the least possible risk. Bankers call it "prudent money." Our money isn't our source of life, our energy is. Our money can't buy us happiness but our energy can, when we distribute it properly.

Stress is the destroyer. Medical science has been aware of this fact for some time. They have developed all kinds of pills to combat it: Valium, Librium, Thorazine, Miltown, etc. It seems that most of the people I know in this city are on something or other just to get through their average day. Call them what you will—tranquillizers, downs, mood elevators—they all attack the effect and not the cause. Meditation goes to the source, to the kernel of the cancer of our discontent, and kills the seed of the stress. Only there at the root can the malady be conquered.

Even our language reflects the need to get rid of stress. Relatively new expressions sifting through from the counterculture such as "hang loose," "uptight," "let it all hang out" have been so universally accepted they have become common parlance, simply because they so succinctly express the conditions that they mean to communicate.

Recently Frank McGee, one of our more prestigious TV news anchor men, died at the age of fifty-two. His twenty-year-old son gave the eulogy, which went something like this: "I know my father was a great man. He devoted so much of himself to his work we never had a chance to get to know each other." A sad commentary. It is too late now for that young man and his father, but perhaps he will have learned a sad lesson when his time to become a father arrives. Will we ever learn to make time —take time—here and now for what *is* here and now instead of putting things off for the tomorrows that may never come? We are losing sight of the all-precious present moment to pay advance premiums for a future that never comes. One of the major purposes (and in my case, results) of TM is to make one aware of "being" NOW, not "to be" later or "have been" before, but "being" NOW. To paraphrase an old Benjamin Franklin homily that if we watch over our pennies, the dollars will take care of themselves: we must watch over, be aware of, our NOWS and our future years will take care of themselves.

There is a word that the great structural iconoclast Buckminster Fuller uses called "synergism." Webster's

defines it as "the simultaneous action of separate agen-
cies which, together, have greater total effect than the
sum of their individual effects." Fuller defines synergy as
"the behavior of whole systems, unpredicted by knowledge of the component parts or of any subassembly of
components." Fuller cites the example of two basic metals, each with a given tensile strength. Combined, the
tensile strength of these two metals is greater than the
sum total of each component. Why? Because of the interaction of their molecular structure. To translate this
word in terms of human endeavor I quote from Hugh
Kenner's definitive study of Fuller. "Bucky: *Synergy*
means that most people do not know it is possible to get
more out of a system than you put into it; to get, in fact,
more than you pay for."

This is how we should approach the use of our energy.
We must find out what components in our lives combine
and feed back more energy and pleasure than they take and
eliminate those that deplete us—the same with the people
in our lives. Just as some types of food are more nourishing
per volume than others, so it is with our friends and leisure
pastimes. I mean you feel one hell of a lot better after a
game of tennis than you do after a night's boozing it up. Not
only do you feel better physically, but the sense of having
done something constructive with your body instead of
destructive is bound to be psychologically beneficial.

Of all the people I have talked to who practice TM
this is the one area in which they are in accord: they have
begun to reevaluate their life structures; and they have not
only perceived but actually done things, made definitive
moves, to better synergize their energies within their life
style. Some have made drastic changes in their life style
because the self-awareness that one gains through regular
meditation made it impossible for them to continue a way

of life that was making them miserable and also gave them the strength and courage to make the necessary changes. Of course, some people don't need drastic changes in their lives; some people are just naturally more happy than others; and then there are always those troglodytes who would perish if they were exposed to fresh air and sunlight, whom not even the good Lord himself can help, let alone TM.

In relation to energy, meditation is twofold. Through the deep rest it gives the body we get more energy; and equally, if not more important, it affords us the conscious awareness to redirect the use of that energy in more positive ways. You might say it acts as a converter or transformer that turns negative into positive.

Brain waves can be measured and alpha waves, which are usually associated with pleasurable input (present in some states of dreaming, and in relaxation with a frequency of eight to thirteen cycles per second). They show we are getting a deep, deep rest, equivalent to eight hours of sleep. Obviously, this increases our energy tremendously. In studies quoted later in this book it has been shown that alpha waves increase during TM and increase the depth of relaxation.

In pursuing the research on TM, I found I was forever, no matter where I looked, running into the statistics and charts compiled by researchers Dr. Robert Keith Wallace (who, at the time these studies were conducted, was an independent researcher but is now president of Maharishi International University, Los Angeles, California) and Dr. Herbert Benson, who graduated from Harvard Medical School in 1961. Grants from the National Institute of Health supported their work. Wallace wrote his doctoral thesis on TM in 1970. Benson is an internist and cardiologist specializing in hypertension, and at this writing is an assistant professor of medicine at Harvard Medical School. I mention them here because I will be referring to their work throughout this book.

Apart from increased energy, another important and measurable benefit of TM concerns stress release. It has been scientifically acknowledged that the degree of electrical resistance of the skin is indicative of the level of anxiety that one is experiencing. In moments of fear and/or tension I'm sure we have all broken out in a cold sweat, as the saying goes. When we are going through such an anxiety-causing time our skin resistance is said to be low. When we are in a nonanxious state our skin resistance is high. Both the Benson and Wallace studies and the Orme-Johnson (more on Orme-Johnson later) research in these areas show that TM reduces our anxiety level by raising our skin resistance not only during meditation but by sustaining a less anxious level for some time after meditating.

Lactate is an acid found in the blood stream. Too much lactate reduces the necessary flow of oxygen into the blood stream and hence into the muscles and other oxygen-needy parts of the body. High levels of lactate in the blood are also associated with anxiety. People with anxiety neuroses show increased blood lactate in stressful circumstances. When lactate is infused into the blood of normal subjects it causes anxiety symptoms to occur. And conversely, peaceful, tranquil people show low levels of blood lactate. The results of Benson and Wallace studies reveal a decided drop in lactate blood levels during and after meditation.

Since TM reduces the concentration of lactate in the blood, it thereby decreases the possibility of attacks caused by high blood pressure, anxiety neurosis and anxiety attacks. TM serves as an auxiliary steam valve to let that excess anxiety spout off harmlessly instead of poisoning the system with bad juices.

Chart 2: DECREASED ANXIETY

INSTITUTE FOR PERSONALITY AND ABILITY TESTING ANXIETY SCALE

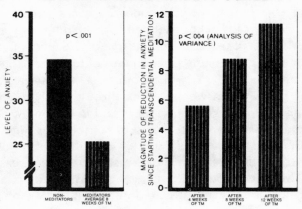

The skin resistance of people who practice TM is higher than those who don't (all other things being equal). That is, in terms of living, you can cope better with stressful situations without blowing your stack because TM relaxes you, enabling you to deal more coolly with your problems and maintain your emotional equilibrium.

The concensus of the studies indicate that long-term practitioners of TM have the lowest anxiety levels even though they may have been among the highest before they started TM, definitely indicating that TM has a cumulative beneficial effect upon the subject.

Other research by Tom Routt of the Huxley College of Environmental Studies indicates improved state of restfulness on the heart activity even after the period of meditating is over because of the superior rest obtained during

Chart 3: **INCREASED PSYCHOLOGICAL HEALTH**

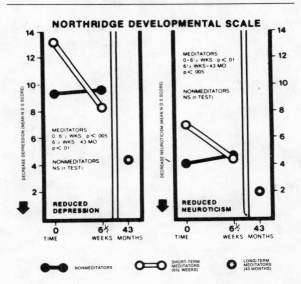

Even after meditating the stability gained during meditating continues to be maintained, building up more resistance to the hassles and stresses of your everyday existence. It is also helpful in preventing psychosomatic illness and increases the efficiency of the nervous system as a whole.

the meditation, meaning less wear and tear on the cardio-vascular system.

As long as I'm going to include actual case studies in this book, I may as well start with my own to show a case in point of energy and stress.

I was invited to Nantucket over Memorial Day weekend to visit with Frances and David, two friends of mine of fifteen years standing. They had chartered a plane that was

Chart 4: **REHABILITATION OF PRISONERS III**

Sociological Measure of Improvement

**Reduced Anxiety, Reduced Offense,
Increased Positive Behavior**

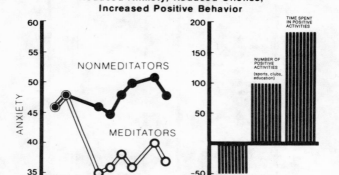

*The results of the following chart produced by a different
team of researchers than those who concluded the data in
above charts and using different methodology also indicate
a decrease in anxiety levels of meditators as opposed to
non-meditators, which also attests to the cumulative benefits of continued practice of TM.*

*There is also a decided drop in the heart workload
during meditation which should be extremely beneficial
for anyone with cardiac difficulties.*

to pick us up at the Marine Terminal at LaGuardia Airport
at 1:30 on a Friday afternoon. The day was overcast. We left
their Manhattan townhouse in plenty of time just in case we
got caught in holiday traffic and arrived at our destination
one hour ahead of our scheduled departure. No problem.

Chart 5: **CHANGE IN CARDIAC OUTPUT**

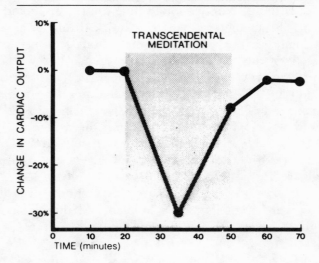

I noted earlier in this chapter that stress/tension is or can be a killer. Heart trouble is our number one enemy in this country today. Therefore the following chart on the effect of TM on the heart function should prove vitally interesting.

None of us had had anything to eat so we went to a food stand and got a hotdog and a cup of coffee.

By the time we finished and returned to the waiting room a call was coming in for us from the charter plane pilot. He had returned to Boston on account of the weather and would not be able to pick us up. We raced to Air New England to book reservations on their next flight at 4:30 only to be told that the flight was booked solid, and we were put on standby and told to report back at 3:30.

That left us barely enough time to grab a cab and tear over to the main terminal for a quick drink—for purely medicinal reasons, I assure you, since none of us is keen on flying. First the cab driver got lost; then, when we finally found the main terminal, the bar was so crowded we couldn't find a seat. We went to three different bars before we managed to find a table and order a quickie. By the time the waitress served us we had to bolt the drinks and race back to Air New England at the Marine Terminal. The second cab driver was another bummer. He got lost on the way back. By now the weather was really bad.

Luckily they had added another section to the flight and we were ticketed on the 4:30 plane. All three of us gave a sigh of relief. *Everything* was late on account of the weather and we couldn't even board until 4:50. Frances began to get visibly nervous when she saw the socked-in field and the size of the plane. It wasn't the usual DC3, but a small twin-engine Beechcraft 99.

Everyone boarded, and the plane taxied to the end of the feeder runway, preparatory to takeoff. Then we sat and we sat and we sat . . . for two hours, waiting for clearance. I stole the opportunity to meditate. (Before boarding David had had to phone Nantucket every time our plans changed, because we were being met at the airport by a friend of his and David didn't want him to have to wait all that time.)

Finally the pilot announced, "Sorry folks, but we have been notified by control that no planes are being given takeoff clearance and I'm afraid we will have to taxi back to the terminal and deplane."

We all groaned in disappointment. All during this ordeal I tried to amuse both David and Frances who were getting more nervous by the minute. Ordinarily under the same circumstances I would have been one jump ahead of a fit, but today I was accepting the uncontrollable situation with extraordinary equanimity. At last, a little after 8:00 P.M., we did take off. The weather had lifted enough to get us out but we were in flight for only a few minutes before the pilot again got on the loudspeaker to announce that our nonstop flight to Nantucket was to be rerouted to Martha's Vineyard because of a thunderstorm in the area and that "other" transportation would be arranged for us.

This time not only loud but angry groans arose from the passengers. By now lightning and thunder surrounded us. David's tan had turned flour-colored and his eyes were riveted to the window. Frances was digging her fingernails into my arm—thinking it was the arm of her seat.

An authoritative gentleman passenger ascertained that none of us wanted to go to Martha's Vineyard and sent a strongly worded note to the pilot indicating our desires. The pilot in turn notified the terminal dispatcher, and after much back and forth on the radio, finally reported we were clear to land at Nantucket after all. Through it all I kept reminding Frances and David about more amusing times we had had in our travels over the years.

We landed without further incident. After we got unpacked I suggested taking them out for a quiet dinner but they both pleaded exhaustion, physical and emotional, after our trying journey. I went to my room and worked for a few hours before slipping off to the sound of the soft rain on my windowpane. The weekend was depressingly cold and rainy as only June in Nantucket can sometimes be, which meant that we spent a great part of it indoors. In the course of our incarceration a discussion of my book and Transcendental Meditation came up during Sunday brunch.

Frances said, "Well Pat, David and I have known you many years and you know we have always loved you even though we did call you 'The Terrible Tempered Mrs. Bang.' But now you are a model of tranquillity, a joy to be around. What the hell happened? If that's what meditation has done for you, I'm signing up tomorrow.'' David agreed, he couldn't get over the change in me.

At the time I pooh-poohed their giving all the credit for my changed personality to TM. After all, I am just as capable of inner growth and tempering with age as the next person. And I argued the point with them right then and there.

But they stuck to their guns. David said, ''Pat, we probably know you as well as anyone, and I can tell you and I'm sure Frances will agree with me, one year ago, had the same situation existed, the delayed flight, the uncertainty of getting out of there at all, the filthy weather, the possibility of having to spend the night at the Vineyard instead of coming directly here would have devastated you. You would have infected the entire planeful of people with your anger and disappointment and fear. As it was, you were the pillar of calm that certainly made the trip for Frances and me a delight instead of a disaster.''

Unused as I am to such flowering compliments I'm sure I turned crimson. I said, ''Oh, come on, that's laying it on a bit thick, wouldn't you say . . . ?''

Frances chimed in, ''Nope, not a bit. He's absolutely right. You would have made a dozen scenes and caused such a hullabaloo you'd have made us all ten times more nervous than we were. I can tell, you really have changed, and it's something more than just being a year older. Your whole demeanor is different. You're a much calmer person and I'm sure that the meditating has done it for you because, let's face it, the rest of your life hasn't changed that much. . . .''

I acquiesced to the point where I admitted that maybe

it was a combination of things including TM. They both said, "Whatever it is, don't change it. You seem to be a much happier person for it."

After I returned to New York they phoned to tell me that they had both signed up for TM.

I gave it a good deal of thought after my return. Had TM made all that difference? In the few weeks after that incident I had the occasion to see some other old friends of mine that keep in constant touch, and I asked them if they thought I had changed at all. They seemed to agree with David and Frances, I am much calmer and easier to be around than I used to be. We discussed it at length and the only great variable in my life now as opposed to, say, a year ago is TM. So, for whatever that's worth, I have to take their word for it, since who knows you better than your old friends?

Being as objective as I can be about myself, I actually am less anxious, or, I should say, feel that I have less anxiety in general about practically anything I can think of. Although I wasn't driving I was in a slight auto accident not so long ago. Both the drivers and other occupants of the two cars involved were extremely excited after the crash even though no one was badly injured. I was the only one who stayed cool through it all. It's always hard to know how many different factors are involved in any one given situation, since we don't live our lives as scientific tests and keep scientific data on all our actions, but I know damned well that in the past few months I have made several life-important decisions that have been hanging over me for some time that I was either too insecure or too confused to make before. At this point in time I am not absolutely sure that they are the right decisions but at least I have made a move and have eliminated that terrible rending apart that indecision can cause in one's life. Maybe in time, without benefit of TM, I would have made the moves anyhow, but somehow I feel the meditation has removed a certain static quality that was holding back my life's progress. You can say, where is the proof? I used to say that to my theologian grandfather when we would get down to the nitty-gritty about God in our theophilosophical discussions. In the final analysis he would always answer, "You must have faith; only then do you find the proof! Remember that, first faith, then proof will follow."

SLEEP

6

To sleep, perchance to dream . . .
            WILLIAM SHAKESPEARE

SLEEP has never been a bugaboo for me. Just point me
toward the bed and I'm generally good for nine hours.
My friends have said the Russian Army could march
through my bedroom in hobnail boots and it wouldn't dis-
turb me. I can, however, remember a few, very rare times
in my life that I couldn't get to sleep for one reason or
another and can sympathize with people who have a sleep
problem. It can be pure hell, particularly if you have to get
up in the morning and function.

Over the centuries there have been countless methods
employed by insomniacs to get to sleep, from counting
sheep to the old rubber mallet, but sometimes nothing
helps. Insomnia is a curse if you are unfortunate enough to
be afflicted. It can destroy your entire life. We need sleep.
Different people have different requirements but we all
need a certain amount of sleep, some more, some less.
Edison caught his sleep in catnaps that seemed to suffice for

him. Sailors take it four hours on, four hours off. Swing-shift workers do it during the day. Today's twentieth-century salesmen complain bitterly about jet-lag interfering with their sleep. God knows how Dr. Kissinger copes with the problem.

Sleeping pills are a dangerous habit. More than one of my friends has inadvertently committed suicide by taking sleeping pills after a heavy night's drinking, not to mention several well-known celebrities like Dorothy Kilgallen, Diana Barrymore, and scores of others. There is no substitute for natural sleep.

I can remember years ago talking to a friend about sleep. She was an insomniac. She was also married to a du Pont. She told me the story about one of the patriarchs of the family who was also one of their greatest scientists. He loved his work but he also loved spending time with his family and friends. Eight hours sleep interfered greatly with both. He started a very comprehensive and expensive research program at the du Pont laboratory with all the talent and resources of his vast company at his disposal. The goal was to try to find a formula that would eliminate the necessity for sleep. One entire laboratory was full of cranky and irritable rats groggy from being kept awake night after night.

Finally, after considerable expenditure of time, money and rats, their results were conclusive. There was no way to go without sleep! The body needs sleep because during the course of sleep a chemical reaction occurs in the cells involving nitrogen (a process I never fully understood and therefore can't explain here) and, try as they might, they could not find an artificial means of reproducing the same cellular action.

Stress is a major factor in not being able to sleep. That's why some people swear by hot milk before bedtime. It is a muscle relaxer. However, some of our stresses are too deep for a truckload of hot milk to get rid of.

In relation to sleep, one thing I can vouch for as a meditator is this. Sometimes when it does take me a while to get to sleep, it is due to the fact that I usually leave a lot of things unfinished during the work day and thinking about these things left hanging over till the next day gives me cause for concern. The added energy I derive from meditation gives me the strength to finish more projects during the course of the day, and hence fewer are left over to keep me awake. That's a tremendous help. There is a phrase that occurs and recurs throughout Sufi literature, something along the lines that mankind "sleeps in a nightmare of unfulfillment." The Sufis may not have meant sleep in a literal sense, but the phrase still fits. Meditation helps us be more productive and alleviates that nightmare of unfulfillment of which the Sufis speak.

How does TM affect our sleep? Well, let's approach that question from another angle: What doesn't affect our sleep?

Anxiety affects our ability to sleep. Unsolved problems interfere with getting to sleep.

Tension affects our ability to sleep. Stiff necks, bad backs, headaches, all caused by hypertension, keep us awake.

Being overtired affects our ability to sleep. How many times does somebody resort to a sleeping pill because he or she is *too* tired to go to sleep? Too exhausted to relax properly and let it happen.

Excitement keeps us awake. As a child if I was going on a trip the following day I could not get to sleep. I still can't. If you are getting married the next day (for the first time, at least), I'll bet both bride and groom have one hell of a time slipping off to dreamland immediately.

If you are going to start a new job tomorrow or go to a new school it might well cause you some anxious moments before you get to sleep. Not to mention having some doubts about getting through the night when the first son and heir is due to arrive any minute.

Then there are any number of outside influences over which one has little or no control: the neighbor's new pup; the drunken revelers outside your window; the party across the hall; the upstairs flamenco dancers; the fire down the block; or the burglar alarm that got set off by somebody's cat. Whatever the reason, it's a bitch when you can't get to sleep, especially when you have to be up at the crack of dawn for a heavy day at the office. We need our sleep. We have to get enough sleep or our world soon falls apart in practically every area. Sure some people require less than others but whatever that requirement is, it is urgent that we get enough.

Besides knockout drops and rubber mallets, the ingenious Russians have come up with another way; they have developed a sleep machine, Somniatron or what they call "electrosleep," that for a short time allows people to get along with less sleep than one usually needs. This machine, likened to an audio generator, sends current through you by means of electrodes attached to the skull and forehead for about half an hour. This allows the subject to relax enough to get to sleep. However, the quality of sleep derived from this process is delta-wave, non-dreaming sleep. There's the rub or, shall we say, the bug in it. It is necessary and healthy to dream a certain amount; and if you don't do it while you sleep you do it while you are awake, which, as you can imagine, could cause no end of difficulties in your daily life. For instance, what if you were a surgeon performing a delicate brain operation and in the middle of it you started to dream? It could prove rather embarrassing, to say the least. Or how about starting to dream in the midst of a bank robbery or bombing mission?

Anyhow, true to our American parochial caution against accepting any other country's scientific advances without extensive testing, one can only get these Somnia-tron machines if he is a qualified researcher and not just an ordinary insomniac. So American insomniacs will have to do without electrosleep for a while.

As I keep stressing, TM is not a cure-all for anything, including problems with sleeping, but it certainly can help in some areas. What it can and does do, if one meditates properly and regularly, is give you that added deep state of rest twice a day so that by the time you get to bed at night you are not too tired to go to sleep. In the Benson, Wallace and Wilson studies entitled "A Wakeful Hypometabolic Physiologic State" published in the *American Journal of Physiology* it was shown that the oxygen consumption of a meditator was lowered (after twenty to thirty minutes of meditation) to a degree that was ordinarily reached only after six or seven hours sleep. That means the body experienced a profound rest during this brief period. Multiply that deep rest by two if you meditate twice a day and you can see why you wouldn't be dog tired at the end of the day. It also stands to reason, obviously, that if you are getting the equivalent of deep rest twice a day, you are going to need less sleep in general, which is one of the most terrific bonuses of TM, since it allows the meditator more free time to, well, just *live!*

Verifications of this data on the profound rest reached through meditating have been corroborated by other researchers using various other methods. (See charts at end of chapter.) In addition to the oxygen consumption test, the change in breath rate also attests to a more relaxed nervous system through meditating, according to Benson and Wallace.

Chart 6: **FASTER RECOVERY FROM SLEEP DEPRIVATION**

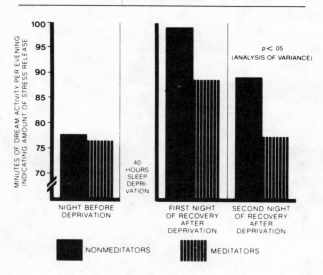

There is a marked decrease of both oxygen consumption and metabolic rate during meditation, which provides the body with as deep a state of rest as eight hours sleep, in only twenty minutes.

What I'm saying is: don't give up your hot milk before bedtime, just add TM to it.

Sleep is a much more important subject in our lives than I had ever given it credit for, simply because it has never loomed too large on *my* problem sphere. But at all the TM introductory lectures, instruction sessions, advanced lectures and even residence courses the subject seems to come up constantly. After listening intently to these discussions involving various types of people in the TM movement, the one thing about which they all seem to concur is that regular meditating seems to normalize the

Chart 7: **RELIEF FROM INSOMNIA**

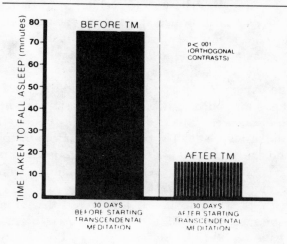

Transcendental meditation significantly reduced the time taken for insomniacs to fall asleep. As a therapy against insomnia, Transcendental Meditation was found to be: simple to administer; immediately effective; stable over time; and without unfavorable side effects.

sleep function. If you were formerly sleeping too much *or* too little, TM acts as a regulator.

Dr. Bernard Glueck is Director of Research at the Institute of Living, which is a psychiatric institution located in Hartford, Connecticut. Because of the findings of other researchers in the physiological and psychological effects of TM, he decided to do a study of his own on his patients.

He divided them into three groups on the basis of age, sex, and self-evaluation (for you psychology buffs, he used the Minnesota Multi-Phase Personality Inventory) to insure as much similarity as possible.

One group was taught TM by a qualified TM teacher. Another group was shown the technique of biofeedback where they could produce alpha waves at will (to enable them to relax), and the third group was taught a skeletal-muscle relaxing technique that is commonly used in psychiatry to help patients relax.

The experiment was done on a voluntary basis; each patient had the choice of dropping out or staying with it. By the end of one year Glueck found the only people remaining in the test were the TM practitioners. Both the biofeedback and the skeletal-muscle relaxing groups had become bored or felt they weren't relaxing enough to warrant continuing their respective techniques.

In the TM group it was discovered that after three weeks of meditating all the patients used in the study could have nightly sedative medications discontinued. Insomniacs were able to get a full night's sleep without sedation.

Dr. Glueck's studies are ongoing at this writing so the final results of his tests are not available until he releases them for publication. However, if you are interested, by the time this book is in print his complete data should be available. His research is part of a task force study being conducted by the American Psychiatry Association under the chairmanship of Dr. James Morgan.

☐ Marguerite Kent is a very rich, very beautiful divorcée who admits to being fifty-eight. Her wealthy, loving, faithful husband of almost twenty years left her ten years ago for a younger woman. It almost destroyed Marguerite, both physically and emotionally. When she became aware that her marriage was on the rocks and there was nothing she could do about it, she practically became blind overnight. Her vision went from twenty-twenty to acute short-sightedness requiring bifocals. She developed polyps in the uterus that required surgery. And worst of all, she developed a tragic case of insomnia.

In the past ten years she has tried every remedy known to man to get a good night's sleep: sleeping pills, psychiatry, hypnosis, giving up coffee, a strict regimen of exercises and country walks, yoga, travel, and new lovers. Nothing short of a wooden mallet helped. Her health suffered from lack of sleep. Her looks deteriorated. Her normally buoyant personality and happy outlook on life diminished. She suffered terrible depressions because she simply couldn't get enough sleep. She even tried changing her life around to the extent that for a few months she stayed up all night, thinking that she might be able to sleep in the daytime. That didn't work. Among other things it interfered with her charity work.

In the interview she said, "I've seen so many Captain Kangaroos and early morning kids' cartoons I could write the scripts." She laughed when she said it but it was too pathetic to be funny.

"Finally, finally, when I was just about at my wits' end, a dear friend of mine spoke to me one day over a year ago about TM. I was naturally hesitant and negative. By that I mean I had tried one of those mind science courses, or whatever the devil it was called, in desperation and all it did for me was to relieve me of three thousand dollars which kept me awake even more, worrying not so much about the money but about the fact that they were making a sucker out of me. They'd still be clipping me if I hadn't stopped it.

"Anyhow, my dear friend assured me that TM was nothing like that. The most I could lose was a hundred and twenty-five dollars [Even the cost of TM has been affected by inflation.]. Then I found out from him that one had to attend the lectures and classes in a group. There was no individual instruction available except for the initiation. I balked at that."

She threw her head back and laughed. "I said, 'Darling boy, you know how I hate group *anythings.*' Anyhow, he promised to go with me and take the course himself, that's how worried he was about me. Well, the upshot was we went to that dreadful hotel in the West Forties with all those people and he *made* me stick it out for all six sessions. I really didn't understand too much of what they were talking about, like cosmic consciousness and diving into my lower consciousness levels, but I did what they told me. And can you believe that after about a week of meditating I started to be able to sleep better?"

She was talking so fast I couldn't have gotten a word in edgewise if I'd tried so I just nodded and let her continue.

"Isn't that miraculous? I sleep like a top now and never felt better."

I questioned her further. "Do you meditate regularly now?"

She smiled coyly. "We-e-e-ll, let's say that when I find myself getting back to the point where I can't sleep I start to meditate again until I can."

☐ Pam Haggerty is one of those soignée career women who came to New York over twenty years ago straight from a small town college. Her whole life is wrapped up in her job and her social life revolves around the people in her world of publishing. She has a country house in the chic part of the Hamptons, a car and two cats. She never married, not because she never had the opportunity but because, in her words, "Why? I've made good money all my life, I never wanted a family nor did I ever feel the need to make a home for some tired businessman. This way, I do what I want, with whom I want and when I want. I've always been liberated in that respect. To tell the truth in a nutshell, I'm too independent to want to assume the responsibilities that a marriage entails."

Ms. Haggerty has been practicing TM for about three years. I asked her, "What made you take up meditation? You seem to have your life pretty well in hand."

"Simple," she said. "I heard meditation gives you more energy. For as long as I can remember I have always been exhausted. As far back as high school I can remember to this day sitting by the hour over a coke in the corner drugstore in my home town with a guy in my class, day after day, and our entire conversation went like this: I'd say 'God, I'm tired.' He'd say, 'Me too.' Of course, we'd been out jitterbugging every night at the local Bar-B-Cue where all the kids met, not to mention the fact that we had all started to drink by then. No wonder we were tired. We never got enough sleep. Besides, I'm a sleeper. I could sleep for twelve hours every night of my life if I didn't have to get up for school or work. College was the same.

"Then when I got to New York and started working it was the same damn thing. Out to dinner, out to the theater, out to a party. Never enough sleep. Who the hell has time in this town to work, play and still get twelve hours sleep? No way. I used to live for the weekends just to get caught up on my sleep. You know, TGIF, Thank-God-It's-Friday department.

"One day, the thought occurred to me that there might be something physically wrong with me so I went to my doctor. He gave me a complete physical, did all kinds of tests, basal metabolism, blood counts, etc. I had to wait about a week for the results of all the tests to get back. At the end of the week I went back to him. 'Well, Doc, what's the matter with me? Why am I so tired unless I sleep half my life away?'

"He beamed, 'Pam, you are a perfect specimen of young American womanhood. The tests show there is absolutely nothing wrong with you. I'm sorry you are so tired.'

"I walked out of his office a hundred dollars and a pint of blood lighter and still exhausted.

"I spoke to my friends about it. Everyone had a different remedy. One said, 'You sleep *too* much, you oversleep. That's the trouble. Try cutting down.' I did. That made me even more tired. I tried pills, ups. They were okay but when they wore off it was disaster.

"I had dinner with a Greek shipping captain and his mistress one night. The subject came up. He said, 'Try goat cheese for three months and all will be well.' I ate so much goat cheese I began to bleat like one but it was a tired bleat. I even went so far as to eat raw liver for breakfast. Have you ever tried *raw liver* for *breakfast?*"

Just the thought of it was nauseating. I said, "No, but I've tried cooked liver for dinner. . . ."

"It's not the same," she said.

She stuck her tongue out. "It's ghastly, just ghastly. Anyhow, this kind of thing went on for years. My sleeping really interfered with my life, like liquor and gambling interfere with people's lives.

"One day I read an article that said Transcendental Meditation gave you energy. At that point in my life I would have tried ground rhino horn. I had just been made vice-president of a new department and I needed all the time I could muster to whip the thing into shape. That meant staying up late nights working and being at the office on time.

"Well, I took the TM course without much hope of the results. I swear to you a miracle happened. Almost immediately, like after three days, I began to get great jolts of natural energy that literally kept me rolling through my

day. I found I could function beautifully on only eight hours
sleep a night.''

I said, ''That's fabulous. From then on you had it
made . . . ?''

She interrupted me. ''No, wait, that's the funny part.
After I began to get used to only eight hours a night I began
to cheat. First I started only meditating once a day. That
lasted about a week and I didn't notice any appreciable
difference. Then I used to miss whole days and finally I
found I had given it up entirely. A meditation dropout.
That lasted about three weeks before it became apparent
that I was slipping back into my need for twelve hours or
I'd be exhausted. That convinced me. I started meditating
regularly again and all was well. Can you believe that now,
after three years of meditating, I can sail through a day and
evening on only six hours sleep? Think how much more I
get accomplished in a day. It's really fantastic.''

Obviously, the less anxiety and tension we take to bed
with us, the sooner we can get to sleep and the sounder,
deeper and more beneficial the rest we derive from it. Or,
as Shakespeare said, ''We are such stuff/As dreams are
made on, and our little life/Is rounded with a sleep.''

WORK

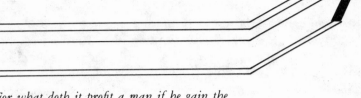

For what doth it profit a man if he gain the
whole world and loseth his soul?

THE BIBLE

IN the dictionary I am using, work has been defined as "serious, purposeful activity, mental or physical." The word "purposeful" implies a goal. What is the goal of our work?

Some people work for the glory of God. Some work for achievement and the accompanying honors. Some work for power. Some work to keep busy. But most people work because they *have* to work to keep themselves and their families in the necessities of life. Some enjoy their work; others hate it. Most are indifferent and merely accept the fact that work is a part of their life like death and taxes. In what category do you fit?

Most of us were brought up in the Puritan work ethic and have been taught that sloth is one of the seven deadly sins. I, for one, cannot go for too long without working or I find guilt creeping in and then I can't enjoy my leisure time. From time to time in my life when I was in the chips, I strove and sometimes succeeded in overcoming those guilt feelings, but then something else happened. I found I missed the sense of achievement, the feedback, that comes from a job well done. No matter how else I chose to spend (waste?) my time that reward was missing. When I missed it enough I would get back to work.

With Henry Ford's invention of the assembly line the pride of workmanship began to disintegrate. Men were turned into robots. Departmentalization was the key to profits. Don't think, just do what you áre paid to do. Just put that screw in that hole for eight hours a day; just add up that column of figures for eight hours a day. That's all, nothing more, nothing less. It was dehumanizing. It cheated a man of his pride. The results were discontent, alcoholism, absenteeism and unionism.

With the advent of the computer age this departmentalism and dehumanization has reached to the higher echelons of the white-collar worker. He doesn't even have a union to protect his job. After twenty loyal years he lives in dread of being "moved up," for fear that it may be the prelude to being "moved out." He lives in terror of a takeover by another company where his job will be considered "redundant." (In common parlance, "You're fired.")

Unless you are high up in the hierarchy of executives or the boss's son-in-law, *you too* can be replaced by a younger man or woman for less money. And in today's white-collar market, a man has a hell of a time changing jobs after forty-plus. Fear and trembling set in. The mortgage on the new house you *had* to buy to keep up with your position is due, the kids have two more years of college, and your insurance premiums have kept your savings to a minimum.

To fully enjoy it and glean the utmost reward from it, you must have the proper attitude about work. Work shouldn't be something that takes you away from your family and keeps you from your leisure pastimes. That third of your day—of your life—spent at work should be as rewarding as the other two thirds. You should derive joy and pleasure as well as money from it. If you don't, you are in the wrong job. Work should contribute to your happiness, and so should the people you work with—and you should contribute to theirs. It is essentially just as much a give-and-take proposition as it is with your spouse, your kids and your friends. The old biblical cliché, "As ye sow, so shall ye reap," still holds. Granted, sometimes ye don't reap all ye've sown. Sometimes some other son-of-a-gun gets it through some quirk of fate, but worry not, tomorrow the wind will change direction and blow some other guy's apples in your yard. That's life. But generally speaking we get out what we put in.

If you are unhappy at work, you may have to make some changes, some adjustments in yourself and your work habits. Perhaps the fault lies in you, dear worker, and not in your company. Is it just you or are your colleagues unhappy too? If so, maybe you can get the firm to effect some changes. If that is impossible it is time to think about changing jobs. You wouldn't dream of spending your life with a spouse who makes your life hell (or would you?); it may be time for a business divorce too.

Now, where does TM come into the picture? Obviously *your* meditating is not going to change your boss's mind about how to run his company. What it does do, as it gradually eliminates your stress, is to make you more aware of what is troubling you—to bring the picture of your work life into focus and clarify it, so that once you recognize that there is a problem, you can do something to rectify it. It also will enable you to better communicate with your employers and fellow workers.

In my own experience, after meditating a few months, I find that I am much more capable of reaching out, of asking for help from other people, in all kinds of areas that hitherto would have been almost impossible for me to do. What has been truly amazing to me is the eagerness with which people respond to being asked for help. They actually seem pleased to be asked and to offer what they can. I was brought up to feel that asking other people for help (without pay) was an imposition. Until recently I never related my own joy at being able to help someone when asked to the fact that *they too* might enjoy helping me.

Another big area where TM has helped in my work is organization. I'm a slow waker, maybe because I sleep so hard, but I have found that after my morning meditation I can really get myself organized and get going on my work immediately, instead of needing five cups of coffee and half a pack of cigarettes. Consequently, I'm finished much earlier in the day and have time for other activities.

But the biggest factor has been my approach to my work. Most of the creative people I know have severe anxieties about their work. Is it good enough? Will other people like it . . . like it enough to buy it? What will the critics say? And the very nature of anxiety hinders one from one's best work. Meditating has lessened these fears considerably, *noticeably,* and as a consquence my work has improved along with my productivity. I am more sure of myself and don't waste as much time trying to second-guess.

Stress has now been recognized by business and industry as a deterent factor in many areas. First and foremost is the incidence of premature death of top management executives in the prime of their business careers. Men and women who have risen on the corporate ladder through diligence and loyalty, who know their jobs and their company through firsthand experience and years of expensive training, are cut down just at the point where they are the most valuable. This is costly, to say the least. It is becoming clearer and clearer to management that something must be done about decreasing the anxiety levels that are causing these deaths. They are searching for anything that will help to remedy the problem.

The American Foundation of the Science of Creative Intelligence (AFSCI) is another branch of Maharishi's movement geared to the business community.

Top-level management, personnel directors and, to be sure, stockholders are very definitely concerned about utilizing their employees to the best possible advantage. They are deeply aware of the effects of absenteeism, alcoholism, job alienation, motivation, productivity, creativity and the physiological and psychological effects of stress and tension on the industrial credit and balance sheet.

High-level representatives of such prestigious industrial giants as IBM, Pitney Bowes, U.S. Steel, International Crating and Container Corporation, J.K. Lasser, Gulf, Westinghouse, Trans-Arabian Pipeline, Arthur D. Little, Inc., and scores of others have been attending the AFSCI symposiums that were co-sponsored by the Chicago Association of Commerce and Industry, the Greater Philadelphia Chamber of Commerce, the Rensselaer Polytechnic Institute of Connecticut, Inc., and the University of Pittsburgh Graduate School of Business.

These venerable names do not bring to mind a bunch of altruistic faddists looking for something to amuse their fellow workers. They are hard-headed businessmen seeking a solution to a problem that is rapidly becoming the scourge of their existence, *stress*. Not a few of them have already adapted an in-company program of meditation and are seeing results in the concrete forms of reduced absenteeism, reduced drug addiction, reduced anxiety levels.

Chart 8: **INCREASED ORDERLINESS OF THINKING I**

Improved Organization of Memory

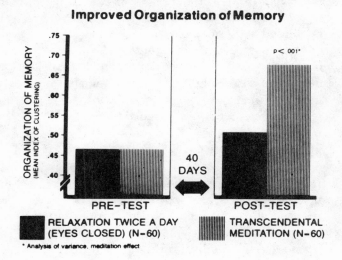

If you do your TM regularly at last—next week you will get organized!

In a TM–Science of Creative Intelligence brochure called "Creative Intelligence in Business," research studies conducted by qualified personnel from the following universities are cited: University of California, University of Cologne (Germany), University of Texas, University of Kansas, Harvard, University of Michigan and a variety of other institutions.

The results of these controlled studies show that meditators as opposed to nonmeditators show:

reduced nervousness
reduced aggression

reduced depression
reduced irritability
decreased inhibition
decreased self-criticism
decreased emotional instability
increased resistance to environmental stress
decreased susceptibility to psychosomatic disease
increased neuromuscular integration
increased perception and reaction time
increased creativity
increased memory
decreased breath rate
reduction in heart workload
beneficial effects on blood pressure
reduced consumption of alcohol, drugs and cigarettes

These are whopping claims and some more cautious researchers dispute the techniques employed and the methods and controls used to produce the above results. However, if even half of what they claim is true, the benefits to a business concern would be astounding. At present, there are over 120 research studies being conducted with TM, all attempting to verify the preliminary studies already reported in various journals.

☐ Peter Kroft has been a successful producer and conductor of industrial shows for the past several years. He is unmarried, lives alone in a beautiful loft apartment in Soho, a forty-four-square-block area of New York City designated for artists' lofts and residences. Originally he comes from a small town in the Midwest. He is in his mid-forties and in his third year of practicing Transcendental Meditation.

I met Peter about two years ago through his next door neighbors who are close friends of mine. Until I started TM I was never aware that he was a meditator. Over the past

Chart 9: INCREASED ORDERLINESS OF THINKING II

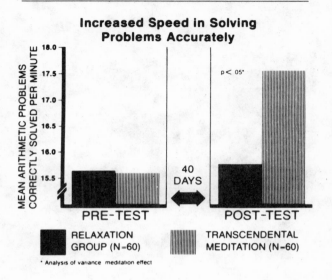

Increased Speed in Solving Problems Accurately

MEAN ARITHMETIC PROBLEMS CORRECTLY SOLVED PER MINUTE

$p < 05^*$

40 DAYS

PRE-TEST   POST-TEST

RELAXATION GROUP (N=60)

TRANSCENDENTAL MEDITATION (N=60)

* Analysis of variance meditation effect

According to a study by D. R. Frew entitled, "Transcendental Meditation and Productivity," there seems to be a strange correlation in all his research that shows TM to be more beneficial for the higher echelon workers than the lowlier production workers. Could be they need it more because they are under more strain and tend to carry more of the weight of responsibility? He also found that meditators experienced more job satisfaction, better performance, improved relationships between supervisors and workers, more job stability and greater productivity. What employer could ask for more?

two years we have met and dined together several times at my friends' home. My impression of him during these occasions was that he was a charming, intelligent, sensitive man with a wry sense of humor. Although he struck me as being

Chart 10: **INCREASED ORDERLINESS OF THINKING III**

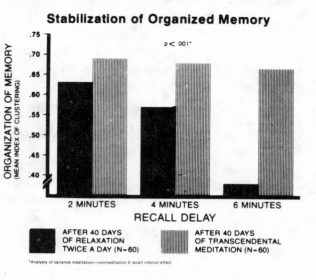

Stabilization of Organized Memory

This study could have been placed in the education chapter as well as the work chapter, as it would certainly benefit students and improve their span of attention.

rather shy I always felt a certain kind of calmness in him that I could never quite explain. When I decided to write this book Peter agreed to give me a few hours of his precious time (when you read what his average month's activities are, you will understand why I call his time precious).

We sat in his loft apartment later that week, sipping coffee and talking about his work life.

"Peter, what *is* your average work week?" I asked.

He grinned and answered, "Well, here goes: As vice

president of TV Industrial Productions I produced approximately four hundred shows last year in about one hundred different locations. My job is to supervise all live and audio-visual dramatizations.

"Last month was typical . . . the early part of the month I flew to Kansas City to put the final touches in producing a two-day sales meeting for an international construction company. This included a two-day meeting using a live cast, four actresses, four actors, an orchestra and nine company executives. Prior to appearing in Kansas City for the *final* rehearsals, I had gone to Kansas City three separate times with a writer and come back to New York and analyzed what the client wanted to accomplish. Then with a book writer and a lyricist, I devised the proper vehicle to communicate the client's message.

"On location we rehearsed for two full days, putting the meeting together, working with the executives, the performers, etc. The show was previewed by the company exec and I was invited to fly to California to recommend a dramatization for the company's meeting in Dallas in June. Together with his boss and a lyricist we flew to California, met with more executives, spent the evening consulting with the lyricist and next morning presented the recommendations to the vice-president in charge of sales. That same day I flew back to New York to attend a meeting with an international vacuum cleaner company to recommend what they might do for their fiftieth anniversary meeting to be held in June. The following day I met with executives from a large farm equipment company to discuss what they might do for a nostalgia party they were holding early in the summer.

"I spent the next few days finalizing scripts, speeches, songs, visuals, etc., for a forthcoming meeting in Miami Beach for a carpet manufacturer.

"Finishing that up, I worked on casting and script

changes for a Japanese electronics company sales dramatization that was also to take place in Miami at the end of April. I then started on an elaborate proposal for an air conditioning manufacturer for a worldwide meeting to take place in Nice, Africa, Spain and Japan and began plans to check on all the facilities, casting, etc., in all those countries."

"All right, Peter," I said. "Here's the big question. It seems to me you had your life fairly well arranged, a lovely apartment, an exciting and rewarding career. Why did you feel the need to start TM or those other methods that you looked into before, Essalen or whatever? What made the search for something else necessary for you?"

He mused over this for a minute before he answered, "Gee, it's hard to be specific but I'll try. You mentioned the words 'fairly well arranged,' maybe it was *too* well arranged. As you know, my job entails a lot of creativity. Well, as far as my boss and our clients were concerned, they were perfectly happy with the results I produced for them. No complaints, in fact, just the contrary. It seemed to me that my work was becoming very uninspired, very unchallenging. I mean, what I'm trying to say is, when you are young and eager and just getting started in your line of work practically everything involved in it *is* challenging, and when you overcome the obstacles and make something creative and lovely out of the initial chaos the satisfaction one derives is terrific. I guess I had arrived at the point where doing an adequate, even good job was as easy as falling off a log. *I* felt that the end results were uninspiring, even though the guys who paid me didn't agree with me. They were thrilled. I felt I was tapped out; that I was more or less doing things by rote. One job, different as the concept of the job may have been, was similar to the next—there were only so many variations on a theme. I couldn't see my productions as terribly inspired, therefore my work began to bore me.

I began to question whether it was just a case of getting in a rut or whether I had in fact run out of juice. Maybe I had the middle-age blahs, I'm not sure, but all I could see ahead of me was more of the same old thing until such time as I dropped dead of boredom or retired. I had lost that sense of myself, that joy of life that makes it all worthwhile. I was on a plateau and couldn't see any way off it. It was about that time in my life when I read about Transcendental Meditation. I went to the introductory lectures and then signed up for the course. I have been meditating ever since. From the very first day that I practiced meditation I began to feel better. The longer I did it the better I felt. My work seemed to flow out of me. My disposition improved a hundred percent. I hadn't known my colleagues thought I was a tyrant until after I had been meditating for several months. I had to go out West to do a show with some people I hadn't worked with for over two years. The promotion manager of the company we were doing the job for said to me, after it was all over, 'Pete, I don't know what you've been up to since we last worked together but you're an entirely changed man. You were really getting to be a son of a bitch to work with.'

"Another thing happened that you might be interested in. I used to be a stickler for being in the office by nine o'clock, even though many times we had worked late into the night. I also made damn sure anyone who worked there with me was on time or else! You can imagine how this went down with the junior executives and production assistants who weren't pulling down my salary. After about a year of meditating I woke up late one morning and didn't get to the office until eleven o'clock. Naturally, no one said anything to me, I was the boss. But I realized how unfair it was to expect my people to work late at night and still be in early without extra compensation. I called a staff meeting and asked them if they would prefer overtime pay for those extra hours or have more freedom about getting to work on their own time. They couldn't believe their ears. They decided on the latter. The upshot of that was we get more work, more creative work, from these same people than ever before, and I wound up a hero. It changed the entire atmosphere of the office. I only brought that example up because I know meditating has made me less rigid. The people who work under me feel freer to offer suggestions, to kick around new ideas that would have been unthinkable before because they were afraid of me. As a consequence we are all a lot happier."

☐ Martin Masmer is forty-six years old. He was educated and trained as an artist. He is vice-president and creative director of a very successful small advertising agency in New York City. An early marriage ended in divorce ten years ago. No children. He considers himself a "liberated bisexual."

Although he comes across as low keyed, he is a highly creative, talented, dynamic man. Three years ago, through the example and prodding of friends, he took up TM to calm his nerves. His colleagues in the agency business were prematurely dropping off like flies from overwork. In his fifteen years with the agency he had saved his money and invested it well. Finances were no problem. His love life was no problem. He is a likable, warm man who has more than his share of good friends.

Until one year ago Martin went to the office five days a week and many a weekend took the remainder of his work home with him to his beautiful country house in Bucks County. Today Martin lives full time in his home in Bucks County. He gave up his apartment in New York. He commutes to the office three days a week. The remainder of the time he spends doing the thing he was trained for, his first love, painting. Recently he had a smashingly successful show at a first-class gallery in New York and sold every picture. More recently he has been made a partner in his advertising company.

I said, "Martin, you seem to have the best of all possible worlds. How did you arrange it?"

He said, "This may sound like bunk to you, but I couldn't have done it without TM."

I said, "How do you mean? Explain."

"Well, I guess I had been meditating for about a year and a half. It didn't happen overnight but I started to feel my life slowly ebbing away. I had just turned forty-three. My career was in great shape, never better. I had no big complaints about my life but there was something wrong. I'd go to my lovely little house in the country on weekends. If I didn't actually carry work home with me, I thought about it constantly. Then I slowly started to paint again for my own pleasure . . . things I wanted to paint. I started experimenting with new techniques and media. By the time I would really get into my ideas I would have to drop them. The weekend was over and it was time to go back to work on Monday. I had begun to do little things myself around my house, like planting and decorating and cooking. I found, more and more, that I was resentful about going back to the city and the rat race and the pace.

"Finally, one Sunday I made up my mind. I was going to talk to the president of my company and see if I couldn't work part-time, a few days a week for a while, to see how it would work.

"The president of my company is a woman. A woman?" he repeated. "A powerhouse is more like it. She works *and* produces twenty-six hours a day, it seems. She never quits. She runs the agency. She writes books. She chairladys committees. She travels. She sells. She cooks and she loves every minute of it. That is her life.

"I was terrified to bring up the subject of only working three days a week. I was prepared to take a cut in salary, but even so she might think I just wanted to goof off.

"Well, much to my surprise and without giving it too much thought, she agreed to try it out with me for a few months. 'Let's see how it works out,' she said. 'If in a few months I am dissatisfied with the work that's coming out of your office we'll decide what to do then. Okay?'

"I was flabbergasted. I thought she might fire me on the spot. She had been known to do rash things when her world was disrupted for lesser reasons.

"I wrapped up the urgent projects on my desk for the remainder of the week. The following Friday I headed for the country feeling like the weight of the world had been taken off my back. I didn't have to be back to the office until Tuesday. From then on I was working three days and off four.

"I had time to really get into my painting. I even took a course in silk-screening, which I did in conjunction with my pictures. It was new and exciting. After a month or so of my new regime I could actually feel myself relaxing, calming down inside. I was a helluva lot happier than I had been in years.

"By the end of three months, which was the time my boss and I had decided for the tryout, we had our meeting. I was dreading the day because I didn't have enough money to live and keep my house without working, and yet I didn't want to give up my home time now that I was used to it. What would I do if she said it wasn't working out for the agency?

"She took me to lunch at one of the fancier restaurants that she usually reserved for entertaining important clients. My heart flopped when she told me where we were dining.

I was positive she was going to let me down nicely and tell me it wasn't working out for her. I'd either have to give up the job completely or lose what I had come to love . . . the time for myself and my own interests.

"She let me sweat it for the first few minutes—she didn't get to be president of her own agency for no reason. Then she asked me how *I* liked the new arrangement. After extolling the virtues and benefits of my new life I slowly ran out of steam. Then I popped the question. 'How do *you* like it?'

"She took another sip of her double vodka Gibson before she smiled and said, 'Martin, I can't believe it. You work half as much as you used to but your ideas are so much fresher, your concepts of the entire campaign so much broader. You seem to be accomplishing more with less effort. You know I liked your work before, tremendously. You were damned good or I wouldn't have kept you this long but now, *now* they are really brilliant. You've got yourself a deal and I'm restoring your salary cut to full pay.'

"That was well over a year ago. I know that gradually my meditation allowed me to become aware of my dissatisfaction with my life-style, and the more aware of it I became the more necessary it was for me to do something to change it, even if it meant losing my job. I had the clarity of thought to make up my mind what was more important in my life and I went ahead and did it."

When I'd finished talking with Martin I had the time to reflect on his story, and it seems to me it illustrates dramatically how the practice of TM allows the person who meditates *to achieve more,* whatever his or her work life is, *with less effort* than before meditation began to take effect in his or her life.

CREATIVITY

8

I swear I think now that everything without
exception has an eternal soul!
The trees have, rotted in the ground! the weeds
of the sea have! the animals!
. . . the substantial words are in the ground
and sea,
They are in the air, they are in you . . .
Air, soil, water, fire—those are words,
I myself am a word with them—my qualities
interpenetrate with theirs . . .
The workmanship of souls is by those inaudible
words of the earth,
The masters know the earth's words and use
them more than audible words.

                                    WALT WHITMAN

Create stems from the Latin word *creatus*. It
means to bring into existence; to invest
with a new form; to produce or bring
about by a course of action; to produce
through imaginative skill.
Webster's New Collegiate Dictionary

Have you ever heard the old adage about "If you want something done fast and well, give the job to a busy man?" Some people get countless tasks accomplished in a day, and other people just aren't able to get anything done. This has to do with many factors, some of which are energy, organization of time and thought, incentive, ability, etc.

Mr. Lincoln said that all men are created equal under God. We may be equal, but we are not alike. Each of us is unique. No two people on earth are the same. We may have look-alikes and act-alikes to some degree but there is always a difference if you look hard enough, even in "identical" twins. To begin with, one was the firstborn.

Some people have known since they were children what they wanted to be when they grew up and accordingly lived their lives with that singularity of purpose. We say these people have "direction," like a single speeding bullet. Others, like myself, are like buckshot, spraying our energies all over the place—jack-of-all-trades, master of none. Both ways of life have their compensations, and both have their drawbacks. My father was a white-collar worker but he loved to fiddle around the house fixing things on weekends. When I was a kid he used to joke about Albert Einstein being a lousy plumber. "Couldn't even fix the johnny in his own house," Dad said.

When we talk about being "creative" we don't necessarily mean that one must be an artist or a writer or a musician. You can be creative around your home. You can lead your children, by your own example, into being creative in all fields of endeavor. In the old days families made their own Christmas decorations and often had to fashion their own toys and grow and can their own food and feed and butcher their own livestock. The people who grew up in those days had a sense of life that is missing in today's culture where all our food is prepackaged, our clothing ready-to-wear and our entertainment from the boob tube. We have lost our sense of life and our sense of belonging to it, of being a part of it. Our children take everything for granted as their due, with no effort on their part beyond going to school and making passing grades. In the old days very few families could afford to have all the children in school. Only the most intellectually worthy were spared to go to school. The others had to stay home and do the chores.

But we can't go back in time. We have to face today's world as do our children and grandchildren. What can be done to recapture the sense of life for them, so that they have some understanding of the phenomena of the seasons and the nature of the universe? How can they learn to feel a part of the universe and not just a useless atrophied appendage, like an ever-aging cog in a machine that will soon be obsolete? Somewhere along the way we have lost the spirit of life without which life becomes gradually meaningless, empty and finally hopeless. Our trust in the democratic system, its leaders and its structure has been misused and defiled from the presidency right on down the line to the local judges. I can remember the time when a man who had judge before his name was the most venerated man in the community; now he is looked at askance—as is practically any man in a political job.

I can almost trace the beginning of this creative atrophy that has set in to the end of the Second World War. All was to be well and cured in the world with our victory over tyranny and oppression. Out with the old, on with the new. The technological advances that evolved from the war took over our lives. Men's minds were told to change. They were programmed to create inferior merchandise and goods because durability of product and fineness of design was not the ultimate goal; obsolescence and profit were the new godheads of industry. Crooked titans of industry, government and unions became the new figureheads for our children to worship—as opposed to those other generations of Americans who were taught that the real reason George Washington became president of this nation was because he didn't tell a lie.

This misuse of our national creativity has finally begun to become apparent to even the most callous. The final results are in: their names are PILLAGE and POLLUTION, not only of our natural resources as a nation but of our spiritual resources as human beings.

If we are to reach the "third consciousness level" that Charles Reich talked about in *The Greening of America,* we had better start now before it's too late.

Every human being has creativity. Look around your home: you created it. If you're the homemaker, you choose the furniture and its place in the room. If you are the cook, you create the meals. You don't serve the same food every day. You create an image of yourself by the way you dress and walk and speak. Some people are more imaginative than others because their minds are more open. They are not afraid of trying new things. Some people are more secure, less fearful of ridicule than others.

It is the concept of Maharishi and his teachers of TM and the Science of Creative Intelligence that the world is not going to change man; man must change himself, and by so doing will change the world and make it better.

Meditation is a way to open up our minds and make them more receptive. There's an old expression about being unable to see the forest for the trees. That implies that we have to get farther away to change our perspective. That's what TM allows us to do. To get away from our minds for a few minutes so that our perspectives, our horizons, change. I've often said, "How stupid of me, why didn't I think of that before?" I was too close to whatever the situation was to be able to see the problem clearly, from all angles. The first astronauts gathered a much different picture of this, our planet, than they had previously conceived, simply by putting more distance between their eyes and the earth. So it is with the mind and our problems. Meditation allows us to clear the mind, to stop thinking for a few minutes every day and to put more distance between ourselves and our ideas so that our mind can get a different viewpoint.

Teachers of meditation don't promise to cure all one's worries and woes, but they do contend that by tapping the inner eye of yourself through meditating you will find a creativeness. You will discover an ability to recognize and change things in yourself and your life—an ability that was lying there dormant, just waiting for you to seek it out. We owe it to ourselves to be all we can be and not leave ourselves to the fate that the German dramatist, Hebbel, describes: "The man I am greets mournfully the man I might have been. . . ."

"TM spontaneously brings the flow of creative intelligence according to the requirement of the meditator," Maharishi says. Well, that's saying a mouthful. I don't think it will make a silk purse out of a sow's ear, nor do I think he means that. We all have our limitations, physically as well as mentally. To oversimplify for the purpose of elucidation, I believe he means merely that we can be more than we are, that TM extends the potential of each person's individual grasp. For instance, the mechanic might well become the inventor if his creative intelligence is allowed to flow—if he combines his mechanical knowledge and experience with his intuition and creative flow.

I never thought I could paint a picture until I was sick in bed and received a set of paints as a gift from a friend.

Granted, I'll never be a Rembrandt, but once I got started I found I enjoyed it and it certainly enlarged my interests and my pleasure in life. It also taught me not to fear what others thought about the picture. It was just for fun and relaxation. The world wasn't going to ridicule me if it wasn't museum quality (which, I might add, it wasn't).

I mean, the lady who invented the Jonny Mop is Dorothy Rogers, the wife of composer Richard Rodgers. The story I heard was that her maid got sick for a week and Mrs. Rodgers had to do the housework at her beautiful home in Westchester County. One day that lovely chore of cleaning the toilet led her to invent the Jonny Mop. She sold the idea for a fortune.

Fred Waring, the late big band leader of the 1940s, probably got tired of slapping ice cubes wrapped up in a towel on the ground to get chopped ice for his guests' frozen daiquiris and decided to invent a machine to make chopped ice in the home—hence the Waring Blender. Creativity doesn't necessarily have to be in a field with which you are familiar, it can be unleashed anywhere if your mind is open.

There is a Sanskrit word called *mahaprajna* which means "great wisdom." I quote a Zen saying: "The brilliancy of great wisdom illumines all beings. To discover or ignore the latent mahaprajna is the individual choice of each person." In other words, it is there lying dormant in each of us somewhere and all the ancient sages propound meditation as the key to unlocking our growth into our inner brilliancy.

Cosmic consciousness or God consciousness—the ability to mirror allows every input to enter equally, reflects each equally and cannot be timed to receive a special kind of input. It does not add anything to the input, and does not turn off repetitive stimuli; it does not focus on any particular aspect of input and return it back and forth, but continuously admits all inputs equally . . . the ability to mirror, to be free of the normal restrictions—of the tuning, biasing, and filtering processes of consciousness—may be part of what is meant by "direct" perception.

Robert Ornstein's words reflect again how our creative force may be freed as never before by reaching a deeper level of consciousness than we have ever known through TM.

Or, as Swami Adbhutananda expresses it in his "Meditation" from *Vedanta for the Western World:*

As one becomes established in the meditative life there comes a control over the mind. Then alone can one know his own mind, how and in what devious ways it works. He becomes immediately aware of any tricks the mind would try to play. The old habits of hatred, jealousy, and all the passions will no longer have the power to raise any wave in the mind.

Many changes come in one who lives the contemplative life. The character becomes transformed, the body also changes, the voice becomes sweet; he breathes differently. A truly meditative man can be recognized by his movements, his face, his eyes. He has wonderful poise, his mind is tranquil.

What is Cosmic Consciousness? "Cosmic" stems from the Greek word *kosmos,* meaning order, universe. Webster's defines it as the extraterrestrial vastness of the universe characterized by greatness, especially in extent, intensity or comprehensiveness—cosmos: an orderly, harmonious, systematic universe.

"Consciousness" is defined by Webster's as the quality

or state of being aware, especially of something within oneself, and it stems from the Latin verb *scire:* to know. It indicates the upper level of mental life of which the person is aware in contrast to the unconscious processes.

Maharishi says, "The significance and purpose of individual life is the same as that of the life of the cosmos. The difference lies in the scale. The individual life is the basic unit of the life of the cosmos." He equates it to the highest level of freedom possible to man. In his "Science of Being" he explains it thus:

> We have seen that during Transcendental Meditation the conscious mind arrives at the transcendental field of absolute Being [what this author refers to as ISNESS]. Here in this field the mind transcends all that is relative, and is to be found in the state of absolute Being. The mind has transcended all limits of the experience of thought and *is left by itself* in a state of pure consciousness. This state of pure consciousness, or the state of absolute, pure Being, is called self-consciousness.
>
> When this self-consciousness is forever maintained, even when the mind emerges from the Transcendant or Meditative state and engages in the field of activity, then self-consciousness attains the status of cosmic consciousness. Self-consciousness is then established eternally in the nature of the mind. Even when the mind is awake, dreaming or in deep sleep, self-consciousness is maintained.

Reaching the state of ISNESS or Cosmic Consciousness is the desired result of TM. It is at this level that Maharishi says one can live 200 percent of life, having inner spiritual fulfillment as well as enjoying the glories of creation.

It has been scientifically proven that there are three physiological and biochemically definable states of consciousness: the first state, awakeness; the second state, dreaming; and the third state, sleeping. (See Benson, Wallace and Wilson chart later on in this chapter.)

Maharishi calls the fourth state of consciousness (see Swinyard, et al.) "Transcendental Consciousness," meaning that through regular meditation "the conscious mind fathoms the deeper levels of the thought process and eventually transcends the subtlest thought to arrive at the state of Being." The Yogis call it *Samadhi* and Zen Buddhists call it *Satori*. After a period of time, when this state of Being is forever opened to awareness, we reach the fifth state of consciousness—Cosmic Consciousness or, as Maharishi calls it, "Bliss Consciousness."

According to authors Senzaki and McCandless, in their book *Buddhism and Zen,* the fifth state is said to be a state of duality; it coexists simultaneously with the first, second, third and fourth states, and this combination is said to equal pure awareness plus a state of activity when you are *experiencing* Cosmic Consciousness. The sixth state is also a state of Cosmic Consciousness that has been distilled, so to speak, to its nth degree. The seventh state is sometimes called God Consciousness or Unity Consciousness where one is in complete sync, or harmony, with the all-perfect universe, or at one with God. "God" is being used here as a poetical expression of universal law—I read this as the verities of the universe and God and man becoming ONE —the natural and perfect circle of human evolution, in all its splendor.

I know I haven't been meditating long enough to reach anything approaching Bliss Consciousness, and I'm not sure how far I am into the fourth state; but as Laura Huxley in "This Timeless Moment" quotes Einstein as saying: "to know [that] what is impenetrable to us really exists, manifesting itself as the highest wisdom and the most radiant beauty . . . *that* knowledge is what matters." I'm sure Einstein refers here to the *Prajnas* Sanskrit definition of wisdom, which has been defined in *Buddhism and Zen* as "that quality of ability to see directly into the true nature of things beyond mere intellection."

I'm damned sure I don't as yet have that kind of wisdom or "freedom from the known" that Krishnamurti speaks of, but if TM is a way of reaching that altered state of consciousness, twenty minutes twice a day is a small price to pay.

To get into the physiological aspects of the effects of TM and creativity we must get into physiological psychology research, a relatively new area of science that is investigating the two sides of the brain, i.e., left and right.

Philosophically this dualism of consciousness is referred to as the "Mind-Body problem." Does the body influence the mind? Does the mind influence the body? How much interaction, if any, is there between the two? Do some people experience more interaction than others? Is that possible? If so, why? Behaviorists, parallelists, interactionists, epiphenomalists, monists, materialists, mentalists, trialists and mysticists have been arguing for centuries over this polarity, and will be for God knows how many more centuries.

As I said, recognition of this duality or lack of it in human consciousness is not new. An ancient Sufi parable, which Ornstein used to explain this issue, goes something like this.

Nasrudin, the boatman, ferrying a pedant across a stretch of rough sea, said something ungrammatical to his passenger.

The scholar replied derisively, "Have you never studied grammar?"

"No," replied Nasrudin.

"In that case," said the scholar, "half your life has been wasted."

A few minutes later the wind increased and the waters became turbulent. Nasrudin turned to the passenger. "Have you ever learned to swim?"

"No. Why?" said the scholar.

Nasrudin replied, "Then ALL your life is wasted. We are sinking!"

I have often heard the left hand referred to as the "dreamer." The Hopi Indians say one hand is for writing and the other for making music. According to Dr. Ornstein, the Mojave Indians say the left hand is passive, the maternal side; the right, the active, paternal side.

To put this in the simplest terms: the left half of the brain is connected, so to speak, with the right side of the body, and vice versa. The left side is believed to deal with linear or analytical thinking, such as verbalization and sequential, logical thinking. It takes in information and digests it and transfers it into language. The right hemisphere of the cerebral cortex is concerned more with interpreting and acting upon input on an intuitive, artistic level.

In other words, to paraphrase Dr. Ornstein, if you damaged the left side of your brain it might not necessarily damage your ability to create music, perform crafts, art, sports, etc. But if you damage the right side it could well impair your ability to perform these functions. On the other hand, damage to the left side of the cerebral cortex would be disastrous if you were a mathematician. It could affect your memory and perhaps give you a speech impairment.

Not only empirical data (see chart regarding a study by J. P. Banquet) but raw data yet to be completely processed and evaluated is leading to the conclusion that meditation

Chart 11

AUTHOR'S CHART DEMONSTRATING ORNSTEIN'S COMPILATIONS OF DIFFERENT SCHOLARS, SECTS, AND RELIGIONS DESCRIBING THE TWO MODES OF CONSCIOUSNESS.

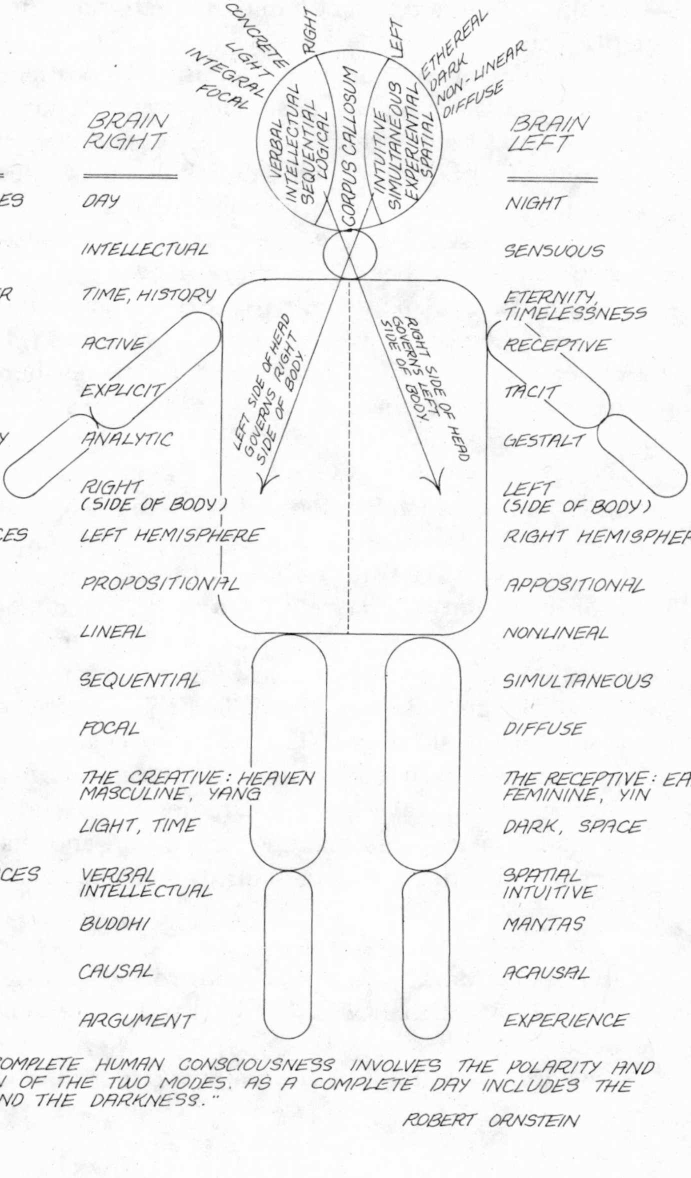

WHO PROPOSED IT?	BRAIN RIGHT	BRAIN LEFT
MANY SOURCES	DAY	NIGHT
BLACKBURN	INTELLECTUAL	SENSUOUS
OPPENHEIMER	TIME, HISTORY	ETERNITY, TIMELESSNESS
DEIKMAN	ACTIVE	RECEPTIVE
POLANYI	EXPLICIT	TACIT
LEVY, SPERRY	ANALYTIC	GESTALT
DOMHOFF	RIGHT (SIDE OF BODY)	LEFT (SIDE OF BODY)
MANY SOURCES	LEFT HEMISPHERE	RIGHT HEMISPHERE
BOGEN	PROPOSITIONAL	APPOSITIONAL
LEE	LINEAL	NONLINEAL
LURIA	SEQUENTIAL	SIMULTANEOUS
SEMMES	FOCAL	DIFFUSE
I CHING	THE CREATIVE: HEAVEN MASCULINE, YANG	THE RECEPTIVE: EARTH FEMININE, YIN
I CHING	LIGHT, TIME	DARK, SPACE
MANY SOURCES	VERBAL INTELLECTUAL	SPATIAL INTUITIVE
VEDANTA	BUDDHI	MANTAS
JUNG	CAUSAL	ACAUSAL
BACON	ARGUMENT	EXPERIENCE

Diagram labels: CONCRETE, LIGHT, INTEGRAL, FOCAL — RIGHT — VERBAL, INTELLECTUAL, SEQUENTIAL, LOGICAL — CORPUS CALLOSUM — INTUITIVE, SIMULTANEOUS, EXPERIENTIAL, SPATIAL — LEFT — ETHEREAL, DARK, NON-LINEAR, DIFFUSE

LEFT SIDE OF HEAD GOVERNS RIGHT SIDE OF BODY

RIGHT SIDE OF HEAD GOVERNS LEFT SIDE OF BODY

"A COMPLETE HUMAN CONSCIOUSNESS INVOLVES THE POLARITY AND INTEGRATION OF THE TWO MODES. AS A COMPLETE DAY INCLUDES THE DAYLIGHT AND THE DARKNESS."

ROBERT ORNSTEIN

is a means of better integrating these two sides of the brain —of making the brain function in closer harmony. Einstein called it "combinatory play."

To be a complete human being, using all our faculties and integrating both sides of us so that they are in harmony, we need to be both architect and builder, otherwise our house will never be completed. For fulfillment we need to get the dreamer and the doer in us together. More and more research is suggesting that meditation may well be the connection we have been searching for.

In other words, in the creative process, it has been said, TM serves to act as a leavening agent—as yeast does with dough, effecting a bridge between the two hemispheres of the brain, linking them and bringing their separate functions into sync.

During meditation EEG findings suggest a fourth state of consciousness which Benson and Wallace call "a wakeful hypometabolic physiologic state" showing high alpha- and occasional theta-wave patterns. Dr. Patricia Carrington and Dr. Harmon Ephron describe in their paper "Meditation as an Adjunct to Psychotherapy" that this state may be an "unusually fluid state of consciousness, partaking of qualities of both sleep and wakefulness." The TM people call it a state of "restful alertness." The following charts may better illustrate what I'm talking about. However, please bear in mind that brain-wave feedback studies are essentially in their infancy, as one researcher pointed out, and that the future research will undoubtedly throw much more light on the subject.

☐ Elizabeth Markey is a thirty-two-year-old housewife who lives in Manhattan with her husband and eight-year-old daughter.

Our interview took place in a pub rather than in her

Chart 12: **INCREASED STRENGTH AND ORDERLINESS OF BRAIN FUNCTIONING I**

Increasing Phase Coherence of the Activity of the Two Cerebral Hemispheres

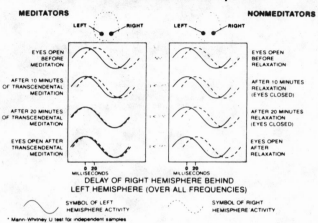

MEDITATORS   NONMEDITATORS

LEFT — RIGHT   LEFT — RIGHT

EYES OPEN
BEFORE
MEDITATION

AFTER 10 MINUTES
OF TRANSCENDENTAL
MEDITATION

AFTER 20 MINUTES
OF TRANSCENDENTAL
MEDITATION

EYES OPEN AFTER
TRANSCENDENTAL
MEDITATION

EYES OPEN
BEFORE
RELAXATION

AFTER 10 MINUTES
RELAXATION
(EYES CLOSED)

AFTER 20 MINUTES
RELAXATION
(EYES CLOSED)

EYES OPEN
AFTER
RELAXATION

0   20
MILLISECONDS

0   20
MILLISECONDS

DELAY OF RIGHT HEMISPHERE BEHIND
LEFT HEMISPHERE (OVER ALL FREQUENCIES)

SYMBOL OF LEFT
HEMISPHERE ACTIVITY

SYMBOL OF RIGHT
HEMISPHERE ACTIVITY

* Mann-Whitney U test for independent samples

*The above chart shows that meditators are more inte-
grated than non-meditators. The left and right sides of the
brain are more closely synchronized, resulting in increased
quality and quantity of creative output. What is art all
about anyhow unless it is to either verbalize or in some
way concretize our intuitions? And that is what these
studies indicate that meditation helps us to do.*

apartment, because "the good fairies from Bloomingdale's
home furnishings department were having their way with
it.

"I met my husband Greg at Ohio State where we were
both students. I was a junior and he was graduating with

Chart 13: INCREASED STRENGTH AND ORDERLINESS OF BRAIN FUNCTIONING II

Increased Stability of Restful Alertness

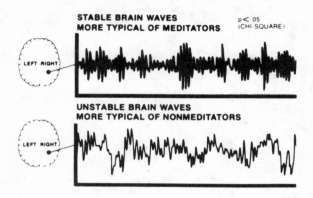

This chart shows different cycle patterns in the brain waves during TM than in other states of consciousness (waking, dreaming, sleeping). While meditating, as the chart indicates, there is a state of restful inner alertness, which is an entirely unique and separate state of consciousness, only recorded in the transcendental meditative state.

honors in engineering. It was love at first sight. Within three months we were married, he was graduated and we moved to New York where Greg had been offered a fantastic job with a large steel company.

"It was none of this 'young couple just getting started routine' in a walk-up Greenwich Village flat. We had it made from the very beginning. Greg was a whiz kid and his company paid him a handsome salary for a young man fresh

Chart 14: INCREASED STRENGTH AND ORDERLINESS OF BRAIN FUNCTIONING III

Equalization of the Activity of the Left and Right Cerebral Hemispheres during Transcendental Meditation

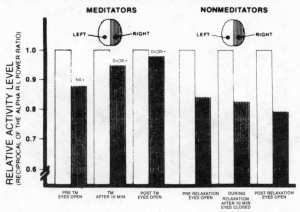

* Difference between TM group and Relaxation group Mann-Whitney U test

God knows, anything that increases the orderliness of our minds can't be all bad, and meditation is manifold in developing our creativity; by releasing stress it enables us to be more coherent in our thoughts and increases the orderliness of our thinking habits, thereby saving energy. The above chart shows that the meditator's brain waves are orderly and less chaotic than during ordinary waking consciousness. Obviously the meditator benefits from the time when the brain waves are more coherent and less random than during non-meditating hours.

out of school. We had a full-time maid from the very beginning.

"At first all that luxury and the thrill of living in New York was very exciting. Greg had a generous expense ac-

Chart 15: **INCREASED STRENGTH AND ORDERLINESS OF BRAIN FUNCTIONING IV**

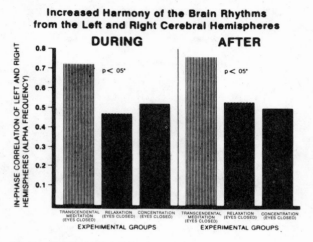

Increased Harmony of the Brain Rhythms from the Left and Right Cerebral Hemispheres

Anyone who has one-track-mind problems take heed!

count that enabled us to entertain business associates lavishly. For a gal fresh off a small farm in Ohio, coming to *this* was something. The novelty hadn't had a chance to wear off before my daughter, Cindy, was born. Then *she* took up all my time and thought.

"But the inevitable happened. Two years ago Cindy became of school age. All of a sudden I was faced with entire days to fill for myself. I went through the usual lunching with friends and shopping bit until I got so bored with looking and listening to those addle-brained women I could have choked them. All we talked about were husbands, kids and who was wearing what to what party. I was getting bored, bored, bored and depressed, depressed, depressed.

"Greg is an angel, but he's very wrapped up in his career. When he got home at night, he was tired. If we didn't have to entertain he was content to have a quiet dinner, watch a little television and go to bed. *I* had just been killing time all day, and that sort of evening didn't appeal to me. I was starved for some excitement—some stimulation, I guess, is a better word. Anyhow, I began to resent the rut I was in and started taking it out on him. For the first time in our marriage we began to fight. It went from bad to worse.

"One of my girl friends had been telling me about TM and saying I should try it. My first reaction was defensive. I was furious. She might as well have told me I was crazy and should see a psychiatrist. A few months later, Greg and I had a knock-down, drag-out fight over the same old thing: I wanted to go out that night and he was tired. The next day I was a wreck. I called her for lunch. We discussed my problems ad nauseum. Finally she convinced me to try meditation. She took me to an introductory lecture at the Wentworth Hotel. I wasn't too impressed but I thought, 'What the hell have I got to lose?' so I signed up for the course.

"Being brought up on a farm, I was raised in the old tradition that anything worth doing is worth doing right, so I stuck to it. That was about two years ago.

"My husband gets a lot of magazines. I had been reading some articles on consciousness-raising groups and seen advocates of them on talk shows but had never given it a second thought in relation to myself. After a few months of meditating I began to notice that I was consciously examining my unhappiness. Something was stirring around in there." She poked her finger against her head and laughed. "You know what I mean?

"Anyhow, shortly after that, one morning when Greg and Cindy had left the house, I started to pick up the phone to make a luncheon date with one of my friends and I stopped myself from dialing halfway through the number. I hung up the phone and asked myself, 'Is this what I want to do with my day, and tomorrow and the next day?' No. Absolutely no.

"I got my tail in a taxi, went to the New School and signed up for a course in Creative Writing. I had majored in English in college. The upshot of all this is I wrote a children's book that is coming out in the fall. I am more pleased with myself than if I had designed the Brooklyn Bridge. My husband and I are getting along like honeymooners, and I'm well-started on my second book, which is under option with my publisher. How's that for a do-it-yourself story?" She sat back in the booth looking like the cat that ate the canary.

I said, "That's great, but how do you know it was TM that did it?"

"You sound just like Greg," she said, smiling. "And I'll tell you the same thing I tell him. Instead of taking up meditation I could have gone to the movies that week I took the course, and I'll bet my bottom the results wouldn't have been the same."

OVERCOMING DESTRUCTIVE HABITS, OR HOW TO BEAT THE DEVIL

9

FIRST, let us define the term as *Webster's Dictionary* does —destructive: a negative agent or force; tearing down; one who or that which causes ruin.

I suppose we have to start out by saying that what might be destructive to one person may not necessarily be destructive to the next, depending upon the circumstances.

My father preached moderation in all things and he practiced what he preached: he drank moderately; he smoked moderately; he ate moderately; he gambled moderately; he drove moderately; he worshiped God moderately; and, according to my mother, he made love moderately. That was *his* way of life.

I did not, repeat, did *not* inherit those traits. I am an immoderate person. As a child, a friend of my mother's who had observed me for years capsulized me by the following: "Whatever Pat does, she does fast, usually wrong and never finishes it." (I got bored easily.)

From the time I was a teenager I overdrank, oversmoked, overgambled, oversped, over-everything except

111

for the things that were good for me, which I *under*did. Perhaps it was a difference in metabolism, generation, environment, intelligence or any number of other reasons or combinations thereof. Had there been more than two ends to the candle, rest assured that I would have burned them all at once. The people I chose as my companions felt and acted the same way I did; more or less. Like gravitates to like. It is supportive, constructively or destructively, as the case may be.

What are some habits we call destructive? From the tip of your tongue the obvious ones roll off: smoking, drinking, drugs and overeating. And then there are some of the not-so-obvious ones.

Neglect of one's health: not getting enough sleep; improper diet; not enough exercise. The major cause of most of our illnesses is that we have allowed our resistance to run down. We can't blame our parents for bad protoplasm if we neglect our bodies.

Is not the inveterate speeder subconsciously looking to self-destruct? Sooner or later he suffers because he is asking for trouble every time he slips behind the wheel. Unfortunately, he usually takes a few innocent people with him. And yet if you told this person he was a potential murderer, he would scoff at you.

What about the compulsive types? There are even some people who are water addicts. They drink sixty or seventy glasses of water a day. They're washing their health away in aqua pura.

And the compulsive gambler: men and women who wreck their homes and the lives of their families. They gamble the food out of the mouths of their children and many times the very roof from over their heads. They deprive themselves and their children of proper education, even necessary medical and dental care. One of the most depressing scenes I have ever viewed is the sight of the haunted faces of the addicts hanging over the gaming tables waiting for their ship to come in.

Then we have the accident prone types: people who are forever getting hurt slipping off stepladders; walking into traffic and getting hit by cars; cutting their fingers cooking dinner; slamming doors on themselves; getting hurt in situations that they felt were beyond their control. These types usually call themselves "unlucky." If you point out to them that their injuries are due to their own carelessness they get angry and say it's not so. Nine times out of ten they didn't make sure the ladder was secure before they started; they were not paying attention to traffic when they stepped off the curb; they were mishandling the knife; they were in too much of a hurry to shut the door slowly. In other words they were subconsciously exposing themselves to danger. They were not taking care. Most accidents don't just "happen," they are caused.

Many times we get into unnecessary trouble because we choose the wrong companions or climate. If we associate with self-destructive people, it tends to rub off on our own lives.

Anything that causes the doer feelings of guilt or anxiety can become self-destructive.

We all know people who constantly set themselves up in situations that are bound to be hurtful. New York is full of women who are forever involving themselves with married men. They spend years waiting for the phone to ring for the few hours the lover can sneak away. The *Back Street* woman then goes through those agonizing hours, days of horrible doubts and fears of rejection and feeling unloved. Anxieties and tensions build. She begins rationalizing in a very self-destructive way. In truth, the man is a cad, he never loved her, and he's not going to leave his wife and family. If she recognized her own patterns, she would see that she invariably chooses to get involved with a married man. So there's really no one to blame but herself.

In other words, sometimes we intentionally project ourselves into what I like to call "Hopeless Situations." If we live beyond our means we are setting ourselves up for terrible anxiety when the bill collectors finally descend.

Then there's the "Mañana Syndrome." When we procrastinate, put things off until tomorrow that *should* have been done today, guilt begins. Leaving things until the last minute puts on pressure. Sooner or later we have to pick up the tab.

To go a little farther afield, we could even touch briefly upon self-destructive actions of an existential nature: ignoring society's mores and laws leaves us open to criticism, ridicule, rejection and even possibly prison or institutional confinement. Albert Einstein once said:

> I have never belonged whole-heartedly to my country or state, to my circle of friends, or even to my own family. Such isolation is sometimes bitter, but I do not regret being cut off from the understanding and sympathy of other men. I lose something by it, to be sure, but I am compensated for it in being rendered independent of the customs, opinions, and prejudices of others, and am not tempted to rest my peace of mind upon such shifting foundations.

Few people are that secure. Most of us poor mortals need the contact, approval and love of other poor mortals like ourselves. So, as we walk through life's garden, we must be careful of whose grass we step on, or else be prepared to pay the price of isolation and the ultimate withholding of other men's sympathy.

Medical science took a long time to recognize that a

healthy body depends a great deal upon a healthy mind. As more and more research data filters in, it is becoming quite apparent that more and more of our illnesses are psychosomatic. Our mental state determines to a great degree which juices flow where or don't flow where. Biochemistry is a relatively new field. However, it is definitely established that our psychoses and neuroses affect our physical well-being.

The late, great President Franklin Delano Roosevelt in an effort to bolster our courage, said, "We have nothing to fear but fear itself." I wonder if he knew the profound and ongoing nature of that statement? If we live with enough fear it can kill us. It's not unhealthy to feel fear toward a wild beast. But what about those phantom fears we can't put our finger on? Those are the ones that gnaw away at our psyches and destroy us, bit by bit. How do we deal with those? They are just as deadly as any wild animal. If we try to ignore them or live with them without searching for a remedy we are being self-destructive.

A recent article in a magazine I picked up at my dentist's office quoted a professor of clinical psychiatry at Columbia as stating that of the estimated 50,000 to 70,000 suicides a year in this country, about eighty percent are committed by people suffering from "depressive illness" which rates it as one of the leading causes of death in America. It is undetermined what percentage of this depression is caused by external crises with which we have lost our ability to cope.

The fat person who has been warned to cut down would object highly if you called him suicidal as he stuffed the last bite of banana split into his gullet. He (or she) might spend fortunes going to fatty farms, buying diet books and diet foods, and the second he loses that twenty pounds, he starts his destructive eating habits all over again. He can give you the caloric count of each and every peanut he pops into his mouth as he eats the whole bagful.

I ran into a man at a residence course in Transcendental Meditation who looked about thirty or forty pounds overweight. I asked him how long he had been meditating and what benefits he thought he was getting from it.

He patted his protruding stomach proudly and said, "Look at this. I've cut back five notches in my belt since I started meditating. Before that I tried the Air Force Diet, the Drinking Man's Diet and all the crazy diets my wife used to come up with from those women's magazines she gets. I'd lose a few pounds and then gain back double. Not only do I love to eat but it's my business. I'm a food broker . . . you know, I sell to wholesalers. I get my food cheaper than wholesale so cost is no object and besides that, my wife's a terrific cook. I usually had a big healthy breakfast, more often than not took my client to a big lunch and then had a good dinner when I got home at night with the family. Believe me, it's damn hard to be in my line of business and not eat."

I asked him if he got into TM to stop eating. "No, that had nothing to do with it. My oldest boy who's in college got started in it and he got me interested. I guess I started meditating just to please him. You see, I've got high blood pressure and he said it would help that. Well, it's funny but after a few months I began to think about myself in a whole different light."

I said, "How do you mean? Can you give me an example?"

He thought for a moment and said, "Yep, I can even remember the day. He and I were out in the backyard playing catch. I used to be a pretty good ballplayer in my day. Anyhow, after a few minutes I got pretty winded and

I don't smoke. My boy said kiddingly, 'Dad, you're getting old.'

"Well, I don't know if it was what he said or the meditation or both but that night I couldn't get it out of my mind. I thought 'Christ, Charley, you're only forty-five and look at yourself. You're so fat you *have* to move like an old man.' "

"So what did you do, go on a crash diet the next day?" I asked him.

"No, it wasn't like that. But the meditation started me thinking a lot more about my life in general. Where was I going? What I wished for in life, etc. And gradually, gradually I began not to have that second helping of mashed potatoes, cut out bread, forgot the dessert. Nothing drastic, no one even noticed. Instead of going into the office Saturday mornings to get caught up, I started to take the wife golfing and fishing with me. The kids, too, if they felt like it. It was like an inner voice inside me said, 'Charley, if you want to live long enough to retire and enjoy all that money you've been working so hard to get, you better lose some weight, relax more, get some exercise.' Well, that was six months ago." He patted his tummy again and said, "I've still got a little to go yet but I'll get there. Every week I lose a little more because every week I need a little less to keep it filled." Then he winked at me and said, "The wife likes it too, she says it brings us closer together."

I laughed and said, "What about your blood pressure?"

"The Doc says I'm normal as apple pie for the first time in years." As I left him he was finishing a yogurt.

Of all the subconscious suicide buttons on our individual instrument panels, I suppose alcohol rates high, if not number one, in our culture. As early as 1869, with the advent of the Prohibition Party, alcohol was recognized as a destroyer of family life by enough people that the most controversial amendment in the history of our Constitution was passed to legally forbid its manufacture and sale. And though we reconsidered and rescinded the law, we have yet to recover from the blows. Prohibition gave the underworld a financial foothold from which to corrupt our political and judicial systems. It is common knowledge that some of our most venerated senior congressmen stay slightly squiffed most of their political lives and are still returned by the electorate year after year. Many a judge who has imposed harsh, heavy sentences on kids with a few dollars worth of marijuana has looked the other way and let off with a slight reproof the boy who "just had one too many, Your Honor."

It has just been in recent years that medical circles and government have begun to view alcoholism as a disease, a form of self-destruction, and look for treatment and cure. Over 100 years have passed since the advent of the Prohibition Party and only recently have we officially recognized that we have a "problem." Socially speaking, there are still hostesses who won't send you an invitation if they know you are AA.

During the research for this book I have encountered and interviewed innumerable students, mostly of college age, who for one reason or another had stopped using drugs and switched to alcohol. Many times the reason was that liquor was more socially and legally acceptable—they were afraid of being caught with drugs. Many admitted that their experiences with alcohol were not as pleasing as with drugs but they needed "something." All of the kids I spoke with who had started meditation had either stopped using alcohol completely or used it so little that it had ceased to be a factor in their lives. None of them said they had returned to drug use. I asked them why, how had TM accomplished that for them? And they answered that after practicing TM for even just a few weeks they found, to use their terminology, "Alcohol brought them down." They didn't seem to need drugs or liquor any longer. More than one said that the "high," the extra perception they used to get from drugs never lasted longer than the time the drug lasted, but the added perception they got from meditation lasted indefinitely. And almost all of them resented the way alcohol made them feel the next day. (How well I understood that!)

Where I come from they used to say, "You get used to hanging if you hang long enough." I know people who have had a hangover every day of their lives. They don't know what it feels like *not* to have one! Or, like the man said, "I didn't know I was sick until I got well."

How do we overcome our destructive habits? That is the big question. First, we must recognize them. It has been said, you can't fight an enemy you can't see. They don't all wear flaming red coats and brass buttons. Nor do they sound the bugle call of attack or shout *"Banzai!"* to warn you of their approach. Some enemies wear the protective coloring of the jungle from which they come and sneak up on you from behind with the stealth and cunning of Cherokee warriors. To see what we are fighting we have to take a really good look at ourselves, and it is not easy to stand back and see yourself objectively.

There are none so blind as those who *will* not see. That's our trouble. We consciously or subconsciously hide things from ourselves. We play games with ourselves. We sometimes do not admit that certain facts about ourselves are true. To become consciously aware of them, to admit to them would mean we would have to take action, to put a stop to our internal enemies.

In Alcoholics Anonymous they ask, "Is alcohol interfering with your life?" It is a good question for us to ask ourselves about practically anything we do—any of our habits—to determine from where our problems stem, to facilitate the search to discover our anxieties in order to conquer them. I remember during the war the succinct phrase "Sighted sub—sank same." First we have to sight the enemy before we can vanquish it.

If we consider our problems as germs inside us, we have to find the proper drug to kill that germ. If penicillin doesn't work then try achromycin or streptomycin or sulfas or whatever. Each variety of germ has its own particular characteristics, and so it is with our problems.

There are many places we can turn for help. If your problem is alcohol there is AA but that only treats the effect. The cause that made you an alcoholic to begin with may still remain long after you stop drinking. For compulsive gamblers there is a Gamblers Anonymous. Again, that may help you to stop gambling, but the reason why you *had* to gamble may still linger on. For the compulsive eater there are any number of clubs you can join, fat farms to visit, diets to follow and doctors who specialize in treating fatties to consult with. But the basic reason why you are a compulsive eater has not been cured.

There are therapists, marriage counselors, consciousness-raising groups, clinics, seminars for practically every malady known to man. But no matter where you turn for help—family, friends, lovers, outside professionals—it always comes back to one person: YOU. You are the one who has to become aware of your inner self. We have to find our "center"—get to know ourselves. What is it that produces unbearable inner conflicts? What makes us want to destroy ourselves by whichever methods we choose?

I have watched a great many friends at one period or

another of their lives racked with inner emotional pain. Many of them have spent years in analysis to no avail. Some died from alcoholism, a few committed suicide the quick way and others are dangerously near the brink. It is pitiful and heartrending to watch. I have hesitantly mentioned *en passant* to some that they ought to look into meditating, but they either act as though they haven't heard me or balk like steers about to be led to the slaughter house and accuse me of being some kind of nut to think that something so simple could help them.

When I say to them that meditating really does alter your state of consciousness, they reply rather fearfully that they don't trust anything that does that. What if they couldn't return to their present state? God forbid they should change their way of thinking about things.

On my first visit to the Museum of Modern Art over twenty-five years ago I remember looking at a painting by Salvador Dali entitled *The Little Known Bird of the Inner Eye.* At the time the painting amused me as did the title. I hadn't thought about it in years until just recently. No wonder he was considered so "far out" in those days. His inner eye was open. He could see through it and project what he saw onto his canvas. He unleashed the full potential of his vision. He saw things with that inner eye that were obscured to people who only use their outer senses.

This is where meditation is so important. It opens a bridge between our inner selves and our outer selves and fuses them together cohesively, but not adhesively in the way that two foreign bodies might be glued together. I wish I could make my troubled friends see that unless they break down those barriers, throw away those intellectually super-imposed blinders that block their line of vision into their finer nature, they will never be free in the true sense of the word. They hang onto their worn out security blankets long after they have become obsolete and full of holes. They have forgotten how to *Live for Life,* for the moment. They express a desire to "be happy," and yet they don't want to change or do anything that might effect that change. They claim to be pragmatists, and yet they tenaciously cling to outmoded and unviable techniques for living.

Among the scientifically proven disciplines and techniques that alter our consciousness, the quickest, least expensive, both physically and emotionally—a completely natural process—is Transcendental Meditation. We have only to open our inner eye to find that cosmic consciousness that puts all life in perspective and order.

In a paper published in the April 15, 1974 *Annals of the New York Academy of Sciences* (vol. 233, pp. 162–173), Swinyard, Chaube and Sutton discuss the effects of TM on alcoholism. After considerable research into all the available studies done not only in this country but in Japan, Sweden, France, Germany, India, etc., they admit, in their final conclusions, that the role TM could possibly play in the total concept of alcoholism must "await further research." They do suggest, however, (1) that "TM might have value in raising one's tolerance to stress before alcoholism develops; (2) that it might help the alcoholics who have already joined AA or attained sobriety through other means to more readily adjust to a life without alcohol."

With most of the alcoholics I know (and unfortunately I know quite a few), particularly the ones who have recently stopped drinking either through AA or their own will power, the big problem after they have stopped is what to do with all that time they used to spend drinking. This poses a drastically serious problem if the person is not, what we call, full of inner resources, used to a creative and productive life.

I was privy just yesterday to a conversation between

two friends of mine who have just stopped drinking. One, a very serious, successful painter, stopped because he realized it was affecting his ability to function in his artistic career and that was more important to him than drinking. The other friend present was just emerging from a serious bout with viral hepatitis and had had to stop drinking for the last three weeks or face the definite possibility of a permanently damaged liver or even death. She is in panic over the thought of a life without any alcohol in it, because most of her adult life has revolved around boozers and bars. The doctor told her that if she continued drinking for another ten years she would be a "liver invalid" (fatty liver) at the age of thirty-five.

I have suggested TM to her as a possible aid in her rehabilitation, but she resists meditation as strongly as the patient I read about in a study done by two doctors, Patricia Carrington, and Harmon S. Ephron. The paper cited a case where it was concluded the therapy patient refused TM because it was seen as a threat to the defense mechanism— just the thought of tranquility is seen as a threat to certain people's lifestyles.

It was extremely interesting to note in the Carrington-Ephron paper more than one case of resistance to the potentially beneficial results gained from practicing meditation. Some patients didn't want to change their self-image, even if it was for the better. One woman in particular had a martyr complex. Her original reason for starting therapy was chronic tension headaches. The therapist suggested TM. After a time of practicing TM she slowly found herself sticking up for her own rights. She complained of this to her psychotherapist, saying that "meditation was making her a hateful person." And even though her headaches had disappeared she stopped meditating because she couldn't assimilate her personality changes. Not everyone can stand getting better! But if we don't start seeking out these supportive ways now it may well be too late. It seems to me that the most precious duty we owe to our life is to enjoy it, not to waste it. A wasted life is the biggest tragedy of all.

My father always said, "When I die, don't put anything fancy on my tombstone. Just say, 'He had a good time!' "

Benson and Wallace, those two researchers whose work I refer to so often in this book, did a study on meditation and drug abuse. They used the questionnaire method on 1,862 subjects, 1,081 males and 781 females ranging in age from fourteen to seventy-eight years. Half were between nineteen and twenty-three years old. The results of this study were presented in the Congressional Record, in a hearing before the Select Committee on Crime, House of Representatives, 92nd Congress, First Session, June 1971.

They concluded that after twenty-one months of practicing TM, over ninety-five percent who had trafficked in drugs had ceased buying and selling them; more than ninety-five percent who had used illegal drugs since starting TM had endeavored to discourage others from using illegal drugs.

Before starting TM over seventy-eight percent used either marijuana and/or hashish in some degree; of that seventy-eight percent, over twenty-two percent were heavy users. After six months of TM, thirty-seven percent continued to use marijuana; after twenty-one months of TM only twelve percent continued use of the drug, and the heavy users dropped from twenty-two percent to one percent. They reported comparable changes in the use of halucinogens (LSD, psilocybin, etc.), barbiturates, amphetamines (speed), narcotics, opiates, alcohol and tobacco.

The results of this study were later questioned because this was a retrospective study based on subjective recall

Chart 16: **REDUCED USE OF ALCOHOL AND CIGARETTES**

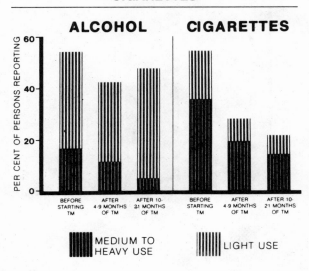

Because meditation does provide a deep rest and reduces the anxiety level, people seem more able to either cut down on or stop altogether their abuse of drugs, alcohol and cigarettes.

through anonymous questionnaire and also because, although the size of the sample was big enough, it was not considered a representative sample of meditators. Why? Because the group of meditators selected was a highly motivated and dedicated group who were attending a month long workshop in teacher training for TM. Also, the subjects were in daily contact with one another, and there was no matched control group for non-meditators for statistical

Chart 17: **REDUCED USE OF NONPRESCRIBED DRUGS**

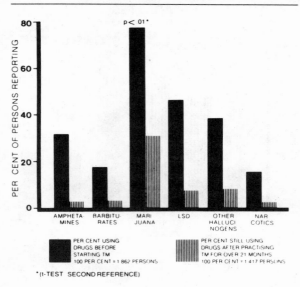

comparison. This was brought to light by another team of researchers: Shafii, Lavely and Jaffe.

Mohammed Shafii was the Assistant Professor of Psychiatry, Children's Psychiatric Hospital, University of Michigan Medical Center, Ann Arbor, Michigan, where Richard Lavely was a medical student and Robert Jaffe was a premedical student.* Apparently not being satisfied with the methodology used by Benson and Wallace, they conducted a study of their own relating to marijuana usage and the effects of TM.

*Dr. Shafii has since become an Associate Professor of Psychiatry and Director of the Ackerly Child Psychiatric Service, Dept. of Psychiatry and Behavioral Sciences, Univ. of Louisville School of Medicine, Louisville, Ky.

They picked their subjects from the Students International Meditation Society's records of 525 TM initiates in the Ann Arbor–Ypsilanti area. Due to the high mobility of the university community they were only able to contact 187. Of these, thirty percent (or 57 persons) had dropped out of TM. Out of the 130 left, 4 did not care to participate, leaving a sample testing of 126. They tried to have each meditating subject recruit their own matched control subject, i.e., a friend or neighbor who would closely tie in with background, race, social strata and way of life of the meditator. Ninety control subjects were found to closely match the 126 meditators. Ninety-eight percent of the meditators and ninety-nine percent of the control subjects were white; there was almost a fifty/fifty match in meditators by gender, with slightly more women in the control group than men; over seventy-five percent in both groups were under thirty years of age. In both groups, approximately twenty-five percent had professional degrees, were fifty-percent Protestant, twenty-percent Catholic and fifteen-percent Jewish.

The questionnaires asked both groups about their usage of marijuana during the four years preceding the test. (It is interesting to mention that the research team went to the trouble to get protection from the Michigan State Department of Health to obtain immunity from subpoena and other legal action to assure the confidentiality for the subjects involved in the tests; otherwise a law enforcement agency could, through court order, obtain and use these records against the subjects and the testers.) All the non-meditating controls answered the question, and 112 meditators responded. Sixty-nine percent of the TM group said they used grass before their initiation to TM, and fifty-one percent of the control group responded accordingly.

The research team felt that the time spent practicing TM might have a difference in the patterns of marijuana use, so they divided the meditators into five sub-groups according to the length of time they had been practicing TM: I, one to three months; II, four to six months; III, seven to twelve months; IV, thirteen to twenty-four months; V, twenty-five to thirty-six months or longer.

The results of the study were as follows. After initiation into TM, during the first three months of meditating, almost half (forty-six percent) decreased or stopped use of marijuana; in contrast, less than one-sixth (fifteen percent) of the control group decreased or stopped. Approximately the same results were recorded in sub-groups II and III. Even more astonishing were the results in sub-groups IV and V, because more than three-quarters (seventy-five percent) of the meditating group decreased or stopped use in this period while only one-sixth of the control group reported decreasing or stopping the use of marijuana.

It is interesting to note that the mean frequency for the meditating group before initiation was 7.3 times per month as opposed to 3.6 as a mean frequency for the control group. Thus, the meditators were using twice as much grass (before initiation) than the non-meditating control group. The meditating groups mean frequency dropped to 2.8 times per month after one to thirty-nine months of TM whereas the control group's mean frequency did not change.

The researchers were interested to know if the meditators could sustain the rate of decrease the longer they meditated. Their final conclusions were that the longer a person meditated the higher the probability of discontinuing the use of marijuana. Ninety-two percent of the meditators of over two years had significantly decreased use and seventy-seven percent had stopped completely.

Shafii et al. also included alcohol, non-prescribed drugs and cigarettes in their questionnaires but their results regarding these unhealthy habits were not, as of this writing, ready for release. However, since the results of their marijuana questionnaire more or less agree with the Benson and Wallace studies it wouldn't be unfair to assume a similar outcome on the reduced use of these other destructive habits.

Dr. Patricia Carrington, a lecturer in the Princeton University Department of Psychology and Dr. Harmon Ephron, Clinical Professor of Psychiatry at the New Jersey College of Medicine and Dentistry whose paper, "Meditation As An Adjunct to Psychotherapy," I've cited above indicated that they did *not* see any decrease in the smoking habits of "heavy smokers" but pointed out that none of their patients had been meditating more than seven months at the time their paper was written, whereas Shafii's subjects who reported a decrease had been meditating much longer, thirteen months or more.

(It might be interesting to note here that this author, due to medical reasons, was told to give up smoking two months ago and did so overnight, and as of this writing has refrained from even one cigarette—and still has her sanity.)

As early as 1971 the Governor's Office of Drug Abuse for the State of Michigan stated that it "supports the efforts of the Students International Meditation Society (TM) as a positive and fruitful alternative to drug use and abuse." They went on to say that they consider the TM program a necessary ingredient to every drug abuse education effort seriously concerned with providing strong and useful alternative life styles for its participants. Major General Davis, Commandant of the Army War College, Carlisle, Pennsylvania has also recommended TM for use in the military drug abuse program.

I feel through my own subjective experience that most people are looking for a way to make their lives happier. Most of us in our adult lives have tried the various forms of lightening our load: through alcohol, the most socially accepted form; drugs, the present-day form for the younger groups; and the "ups" and "downs" that are readily available with a prescription from your family physician to enable you to get through your average tension-ridden days. After a period of time, we must come to realize that all we do is increase the dosage, not eliminate the need. The average person who stays with TM is probably the person with the will to live a better life. Even if the results are seemingly abstract to some, they continue TM because it is a positive gesture that, if nothing else, makes them feel that they have made a step in the right direction twice a day, every day— as though they have done a good deed for *themselves*. It *is* a loving gesture toward oneself, life-sustaining, as it were, and that is bound to be beneficial.

No matter what our self-destructive habits are, we have to approach and become totally aware of their basis, which lies somewhere deep within each of us. Anxiety-tension *can* be helped or eliminated by continuing meditation, depending upon the depth of our problems.

I don't say that we all should change our way of doing things if it suits us and makes us happy. I had a conversation with a friend of mine just recently about this.

Pamela, an English friend of mine from Spain, was visiting me one day and happened to look over the unfinished manuscript of this book. When she finished reading I said, "Well, how do you like it? Does it make you want to learn to meditate?"

Pamela was born in India, spent her childhood there as an English army brat and then moved to Morocco where she spent most of her adult life living among the natives in the remote hill country with her husband, a social anthropologist. She admits to fifty-two and is, to put it mildly, one of the most liberated and, well, "far-out" women I have ever met. As a child in India she learned to smoke grass before she learned to drink.

She burst out laughing. "God, no. I don't want to do anything that's going to change *my* life style. I like my life and I certainly wouldn't want to give up drugs or liquor, as you point out in your book that many people do stop after they begin meditating."

I had to think about that for a minute. At that point I had been meditating about three months.

She said, "Speaking of drugs, how about a smoke? I have some great Moroccan hash. . . ."

I poured us a glass of wine while she stuffed her beautiful ivory-inlaid pipe full of hash and lit up.

I said, taking a deep pull on the pipe, "Three months of meditating doesn't seem to have changed my lifestyle, does it?"

She laughed and said, "Maybe you're doing it wrong or maybe those statistics about people giving up drugs and booze are a lot of balderdash."

That was three months ago. At this writing I have yet to give up either liquor or smoking grass, but something is happening. I have just recently become aware of occasionally turning down a smoke simply because I feel so good and so aware of the pure job of feeling good and healthy and full of new energy that I find I resent coming down from that feeling, which is what grass does to me now. I also find myself becoming more and more resentful of having a hangover from too much alcohol the night before. Hangovers, that feeling of not feeling really good, are beginning to bore me blue, and I don't like it. For the first time in my life, I find I can leave before the last bar closes. I don't like

getting drunk any longer, nor, I find, do I like to spend my
time with people who do—they're beginning to bore me
too.

I'm beginning to think Pamela was right. Meditation
is starting to change *my* lifestyle *and* some of my circle of
friends and acquaintances, whom I am realizing are a waste
of time and energy. But, contrary to Pamela's thinking, I
wonder why I waited this long. As far as I'm concerned, the
change is long overdue. I don't expect at this stage of my
life that I'll ever become a total teetotaler or turn my nose
up at some good Moroccan hash if it comes along, but who
knows? Stranger things have happened! And I have already
eliminated three to four packs of cigarettes from my daily
diet.

PHYSICAL IMPACT

10

I N dealing with this chapter I am reminded of that old song we used to sing around the Girl Scout campfire which goes: "The hip bone is connected to the thigh bone, the thigh bone is connected to the leg bone," and so on and so on. From the top of our head to the tips of our toes we are connected by miles and miles of arteries, blood vessels, muscles, tissues, fibers, nerves, cells, bones, organs, et al. The human body is a highly complicated and delicate mechanism. Sometimes the tiniest imbalance in one area can seriously disrupt or impair the functioning of the entire body. Like one bad apple can spoil the barrel, one bad tooth can poison the entire system. Too much tension and stress in our lives can similarly damage or at least upset the delicate balance of our interconnected parts and vitiate our energy and joy.

Therefore, I have included in this chapter not only the physiological but the biological and psychological impact of TM in its role of releasing tension from the mind and body.

As long ago as 1971 I read an article in *Time* about a

study conducted by Dr. Thomas Holmes, a professor of psychiatry at the University of Washington in Seattle citing the impact of stress on our lives. The timing coincided with the fact that my dentist had told me stress was probably the major cause of my dental problem, so I paid more than my usual attention to it.

He concluded that too many changes in our lives in a short period of time can produce "grave illness" or "abysmal depression." These changes don't necessarily have to be for the worse; i.e., a job change can be for the better, but merely the fact that you change causes a certain amount of adjustment and that in itself can cause tension. On a scale from one to one hundred he assigned so many points to various changes. If you are unfortunate enough to score 300 points in a one-year period, you're in trouble. Using Dr. Holmes's scale for a man like former Attorney General John Mitchell, one should be able to predict some sort of emotional crack-up or physical disaster like a heart attack or stroke, for *his* changes read as follows:

Marital separation	65
Fired at work	47
Retirement	45
Change in financial status	38
Change to different line of work	36
Change in number of arguments with spouse	36
Change in responsibilities at work	29
Revision of personal habits	24
Change in work hours or conditions	20
Change in recreation	19
Change in social activities	18
Change in number of family get-togethers	15

These add up to an ominous grand total of 392. With a conviction, we would have to add sixty-three points for a jail sentence and fifteen more points for a change in eating habits. Now, if Dr. Holmes's theories are correct, John Mitchell would be a "no price" risk even for Lloyd's of London. As yet there is no news that TM ever spread to the "Palace Guard" or the oval room at the White House. Wouldn't hoit, as they say in Brooklyn. Just think how the course of history might have changed if G. Gordon Liddy and the plumbers had taken twenty minutes time out to do their TM *that* night?

There are as many theories about where our traumas, anxieties and neuroses begin and end as there are stars in the galaxy. Some contend the beginning is intrauterine; others say they begin out of the uterus, in the birth canal; others insist that they start postnatally after the actual birth, and more contend that they develop as we go along. Who cares, since it's academic.

The fact remains, if we've got them we have to cope with them and try to get rid of them if for no other reason than that we suffer from them. They affect our lives adversely. And usually they are cumulative. Sometimes the causes of our troubles can be traced, through intensive and expensive therapy. However, if the advocates of intrauterine neurosis are correct, I, for one, would find it difficult to remember back that far, so I have to deal with the here and now as do most of us. Relatively speaking, there are very few desperately serious cases (psychotics) in the world. Most of us are just your average neurotic, give or take, and with a little help and effort and extra insight we can overcome.

A nuclear-powered psychiatric microscope has yet to be invented, so at this juncture in time every avenue of attempted solution is more or less a shot into the darkness of our minds. Or, to borrow a line from a Dorothy Fields–Cy Coleman Broadway musical:

"Where am I going and what will I find,
Here in this grab bag that I call my mind?"

New research into the psycho-physiological impact of meditation upon the mind and body is giving new credence to the ancient claims of the powers of meditating, as the charts and diagrams in this chapter will show.

The Western scientific community has always been slow, if not downright bullheaded, about accepting new theories—even if they have been absolutely proven to be able to instantly relieve human suffering. They laughed at Pasteur, the Curies, Freud, Dr. Ehrlich and his magic bullet (for syphilis), acupuncture, Joseph Lister (discoverer of aseptic surgery) and scores of others who led the way, some of whom died penniless and in ignominy, scoffed out of the scientific world.

I have spoken to some highly respected psychiatrists in New York City about TM and asked if I could interview them for this book. Either they don't know enough about it, or if they do, they are connected closely with certain medical associations that they contend would frown on—if not actually chastise—them for coming out in the cause of meditation, even though they personally thought it has helped their patients. It's that old "let's wait and see" attitude, too chicken to put themselves on the line first. There are, however, a few who have taken the time and trouble to familiarize themselves with meditation and hard data in favor of TM is accumulating. I was actually amazed to read the paper of Dr. Carrington and Dr. Ephron because they are the first I have found to come up with a definitive research study in their "Meditation as an Adjunct to Psychotherapy" that is totally objective. This is true in that they are not involved in the TM movement per se, although they both took up TM merely to better understand and familiarize themselves with their subject matter and their patients.

Unfortunately, to this date most of the basic research has been done by *advocates* of TM: Glueck at the Hartford Institute, Harold Bloomfield, and Wallace and Benson. Therefore, their findings are more subject to a biased outlook.

Even I find myself proselytizing, although I am really trying to be as objective as possible, simply because what I am experiencing as a direct result of meditating is so exciting for me at this stage of my life that it is difficult not to. It has affected practically every area of my existence. My whole outlook on everyday life has slowly, almost imperceptibly, but surely undergone a change for the better. I know that the adverse circumstances that have occured during the past eight months of my life would once have decked me, if not actually put me away somewhere. I mean, everything has gone wrong, all at once. But I have gained a different attitude about the transiency of trouble that I never had before. I know it is going to end, and if I keep my wits about me, all will work out.

Now I'm beginning to look at disaster the way Nasrudin did when his wife heard burglars in their home. She said, "Nasrudin, I hear a burglar downstairs." "Not a sound," he cautioned her. "We have nothing for him to steal and besides, with any luck he might leave something worthwhile behind. . . ."

In the course of writing this and rereading what I have written, I feel a little like the guy who walks down the street trying to give five dollar bills away to passersby. He invariably runs into people who refuse to take them because they can only accept, without skepticism, the misery life has to offer them and not the beautiful gifts.

Anyway, to get back to Doctors Carrington and Ephron, they started their paper on meditating by saying:

In a world where spiritual enrichment from any source is scarce, many patients hunger for a more profound sense of self than is implicit in merely "getting along with others." . . . The use of meditation along with psychotherapy may be an inevitable accompaniment of the latter's trend toward encompassing more and varied aspects of man.

In the Hartford Institute studies on TM, doctors and nurses observed that the meditating patients "had an increased sense of themselves, of their own identity. They (the patients) become increasingly aware of their 'rights' in situations where they had not been aware of them before. They began to stick up for their rights and were less submissive." (Conceivably that might not bode too well with their spouses.)

The Institute's staff more or less concludes that, after several months of meditation, subjects have a clearer sense of their separate identities and a more acute awareness of their own individual needs and rely less on external sources for a "definition of their attitudes, judgments and sentiments and their views of themselves." They sense their "personal rights more strongly" and are less inclined to abandon their own opinions for those of others. And as a consequence they become more decisive, express opinions more openly and disagree with others "where formerly they would have been submissive."

Carrington and Ephron contend that their patients seem to experience emotions after meditating that they would not have prior to meditating, and are better able to express these emotions. This certainly suggests that meditation would be very beneficial to both psychoanalyst and patient by breaking through hitherto impenetrable barriers to understanding. Dr. Glueck describes it as "a new window into the unconscious."

Dr. Carrington and Dr. Ephron agree with Glueck's findings (the latter is conducting experiments with meditators at the Institute for Living in Hartford, Connecticut). They think that immediately after meditating the flow of free association is less full of the sham and role playing of ordinary life and is particularly rich in content, that painful experiences surface more often and are better tolerated by the patient. In some instances disabling creative blocks completely disappear. In other words, the patient is being more truthful with him- or herself in admitting problems.

The effect of meditation on the mood of the patients is up, and a sense of well-being seems to pervade. (The doctors qualify this finding, however, by saying that the mood occurs in patients with low-grade depressions.) In high-grade depressions patients may refuse to meditate or, if they do, rapidly discontinue the practice. They are so unhealthy that they don't want to feel good, whether or not it is from a feeling of guilt, fear of loss of control or a threat to their defensive system. Then there is the patient who thinks that if he or she progresses too rapidly through meditation the doctor may want to get rid of the patient before the patient is ready to get rid of the doctor.

In the experience of Carrington and Ephron, they did not run across any patient who dropped out of psychotherapy because of meditation. My research disagrees with theirs on this point. I have talked with people at the residence course who told me that they stopped seeing a shrink because they didn't feel the tensions and stresses they used to or, if they did, they could more readily deal with them.

They also discovered that some patients who had begun meditation could not stand being unstressed so rapidly from their particular problems. I can compare this experience to a deep sea diver who comes up too fast and gets the bends from the rapid decompression. In this case, the patients couldn't stand getting rid of the problems they had lived with for so long so quickly. The researchers cut down the meditating periods, in some cases to once a week, and that seemed to alleviate the psychological bends that the patient was suffering.

They came across patients who overmeditated. In many cases these were addictive types. They concluded that heavy doses of meditating in a person with an adverse psychiatric history could be contraindicated, because such extended meditation might bring on psychotic symptoms. They did not care to declare themselves about what four or five hours meditation would do to the normal person.

I've never tried more than the prescribed time, but at the Litchfield, Connecticut TM retreat I met a young Harvard undergraduate who admitted to meditating much more than the usual twenty minutes twice a day. He spent more like a couple of hours a day, and he did seem a bit spaced out to me. At the residence courses it is true that they meditate more than the usual two twenty-minute sessions but that is under different conditions in "a controlled environment," meaning that the meditation, exercise and activity has all been taken into consideration and the activities of the entire day are geared accordingly.

Carrington and Ephron found that sometimes just normal meditating makes people so aware of their rights so quickly that it unleashes a great deal of suppressed rage at the world in general or at someone or something specific. The therapists call this a too-rapid release of "emotionally charged material (unstressing reactions)." In one instance they dealt with this type of patient by meditating *with* the patient and dealing with the rage immediately after the meditating period was over and they found this method to be extremely helpful. Although they admit that in their treatment of meditating patients the meditation regimen must sometimes be modified, they do conclude that in some instances TM contributes "in a direct fashion to the patient's therapeutic progress with few, if any, complications."

They also concluded that the personality growth of well integrated people can benefit considerably by TM but they are not sure whether TM could be considered a form of therapy: "it has only limited usefulness as a sole therapeutic agent."

The list of ailments that Drs. Carrington and Ephron consider would be benefited by the practice of meditation are:

Tension states and/or anxiety reactions
Psychophysiologic disorders
Chronic fatigue states
Insomnia and hypersomnias
Abuse of "soft" drugs, alcohol and tobacco
Paranoid tendencies
Obsessive-compulsive tendencies
Chronic low-grade depressions or sub-acute reactive
    depressions
Low frustration tolerance (they suggest use of TM in
    cases of organic as well as psychogenic irritability
    since preliminary observations suggest that medita-
    tion was useful in increasing overall adjustment in
    several isolated cases of brain injury)
Strong submissive trends and/or poorly developed
    psychological differentiation
Blocks to productivity
Inadequate contact with affective life
To shift emphasis with the patient's reliance on self (of
    particular use when terminating long-term psycho-
    therapy or psychoanalysis)

They agree with R. D. Laing in their conclusion that the psychoanalyst himself (herself) could derive great benefits from the practice of meditation and could well make himself more receptive to the communications of his patients.

They expect to see an increase in the number of psychiatric patients who meditate (if the interest and growth in meditation techniques continue at their present rate) and they believe that a "rapprochement between psychiatry and meditation" will bring a "fruitful opportunity for all concerned."

Penal institutions have long been used for many and varied studies because of their (pardon the pun) captive audience, and experiments in TM are no exception. In fact, the very nature of the experiments lends itself to institutionalized subjects, to find out if the practice of TM can indeed lessen their anxieties and be beneficial in their rehabilitation. A series of research studies was carried on in the following penal institutions: Stillwater State Prison, Stillwater, Minnesota; La Tuna Federal Penitentiary; and Lampoc Federal Correction Institution, Lampoc, California.

To capsulize the report and conclusions of the experiment at Stillwater: they used the State Trait Anxiety Inventory (STAI), a measure of momentary and general anxiety. This test was administered over a ten-week period to experimental and control groups. For a two-week period all inmates were locked in their cells. They were not permitted to leave their cells for any reason, not to work, not to shower, nothing. Guards searched their cells for weapons, drugs and other contraband during this period. This produced an unusual state of high anxiety in the inmates and provided a positive check on the sensitivity of the STAI test. The analysis was not complete but the partial results of the test indicated that (1) within a few days of practice the meditation group showed significantly reduced levels of both momentary and general anxiety; (2) the anxiety in the meditators did not show a gradual decline but was reduced quickly and remained at a low level; (3) meditators also reported reduced use of drugs and cigarettes (this was undocumented); and (4) preliminary indications of material not fully analyzed showed supporting evidence of somewhat lowered and more stable blood pressure.

A pilot project at the Federal Correctional Institute at Lampoc, California using the Spielberger State Trait Anxiety Inventory also indicated a lasting reduction of anxiety levels for the meditating group of inmates. They further decided that TM can be taught economically and effectively in the institutional environment. They are hoping to find that anxiety reduction will lead to a commensurate reduction in custodial problems, behavior and drug abuse. They are planning more research to test the effects of TM on aggressive and self-destructive behavior.

At La Tuna Federal Penitentiary a psychological test, Minnesota Multiphasic Personality Inventory (MMPI), was given to inmates before and after two months of TM. The results showed normalization of two personality variables (psychasthenia and social introversion) after two months of meditating. Abnormal values of these are associated with criminal behavior. That led researchers to believe that meditation provides both a physiological and psychological basis for prisoner rehabilitation.

The Santa Clara County Adult Probation Department included TM in its drug diversion program in 1973.

In evaluating the following charts, I think it is important to bear in mind not just the obvious implications in terms of tax dollars that might be saved by the reduction in staff needed to supervise these people whom society has seen fit to incarcerate but also in humanitarian terms, be-

Chart 18: **REHABILITATION OF PRISONERS I**

Physiological Measure of Improvement

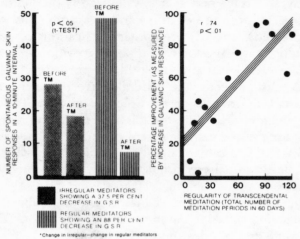

IRREGULAR MEDITATORS
SHOWING A 37.5 PER CENT
DECREASE IN G.S.R.

REGULAR MEDITATORS
SHOWING AN 88 PER CENT
DECREASE IN G.S.R.

*Change in irregular—change in regular meditators

This chart too is fascinating not only due to the extreme difference in the anxiety levels between meditators and non-meditators but because the results could indicate a significant decrease in the amount of supervisory personnel needed. Also, it is possible that these same prisoners who show such marked improvement in their behavior could be moved from the maximum security prisons to more rehabilitative institutions and could conceivably lessen the amount of recidivism, at a saving of untold tax dollars.

cause there but for the grace of God go we. It is one thing for society to protect itself by restricting the presence of these convicted criminals to institutions, but it is another for society to inflict such unnecessary emotional bondage upon them as the undue anxieties that make them worse criminals

Chart 19: **REHABILITATION OF PRISONERS II**

Psychological Measure of Improvement
MINNESOTA MULTIPHASIC PERSONALITY INVENTORY

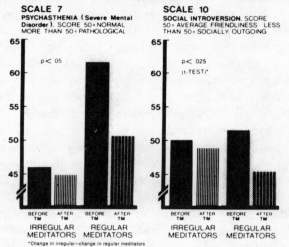

SCALE 7
PSYCHASTHENIA (Severe Mental
Disorder). SCORE 50 = NORMAL
MORE THAN 50 = PATHOLOGICAL

SCALE 10
SOCIAL INTROVERSION. SCORE
50 = AVERAGE FRIENDLINESS LESS
THAN 50 = SOCIALLY OUTGOING

$p < .05$

$p < .025$
(t-TEST)*

BEFORE TM AFTER TM BEFORE TM AFTER TM
IRREGULAR MEDITATORS   REGULAR MEDITATORS
*Change in irregular—change in regular meditators

BEFORE TM AFTER TM BEFORE TM AFTER TM
IRREGULAR MEDITATORS   REGULAR MEDITATORS

Chart 19 shows dramatic results in that the regular practice of TM seems to produce drastically lowered anxiety levels in prisoners suffering from psychasthenia. (Webster describes psychasthenia as a neurotic condition characterized by obsessions, phobias, etc.) In other words, it helps to keep the really restless inmates from going round the bend.

than when they entered the prisons. Therefore, as well as being truly humane for those behind bars, if TM can be used as a rehabilitative therapy for these people it can only benefit society itself in the long run.

This chart is very interesting because not only does it

show that the prisoners who were the most anxious before TM were helped by it the most but it also points out that doing your TM twice a day instead of once almost doubles the amount of stress released.

The Institute for Fitness and Athletics is a division of the American Foundation for the Science for Creative Intelligence that was established to act as a central agency for compiling and disseminating the data and knowledge of SCI to those actively involved "in the development of external and internal methods of physiological perfection of the human body." So they say in the brochure that goes out to physical fitness instructors, ball team managers and owners all over the country, both amateur and professional.

As we all know from reading the headlines in the sports section of the daily newspapers, athletics in this, the latter part of the twentieth century, is a multimillion-dollar business; some pro ballplayers' salaries run well into six figures a year, which isn't exactly chopped liver for a young kid fresh out of college. In fact, nine times out of ten, those first ten years of pro ball are probably the highlight in his professional working career if, *if* he doesn't sustain a bad injury or a series of injuries that keep him from performing his job.

For those gigantic salaries the owners and managers demand peak regular performances. In the old days the approach was much more humanistic. Today, with the enormous amounts of money involved, the plays and strategies are set up with almost scientific computerized precision; specific plays for specific players. If that player happens to be injured, that play has to be scrapped. No team is able to afford two Joe Namaths—if there were two Joe Namaths available.

Because of the prodigious financial stake, these men are treated like expensive machines and expected to produce a given return on the investment. These machines are fed special, extra-energy-producing diets, prescribed rest, extensive training, special doctors and handlers, super protective and expensive equipment, etc. But with all these precautions, because the athlete is human and not mechanical, spare parts are not available. Namath cannot send out for another knee or Walker for another leg. Stay fit is the name of the game, if their careers and their financial security are to be prosperous.

Anyone who has ever participated in contact sports like football or hockey can imagine what it must feel like to be hit and piled upon by half a ton or more of human flesh and bones at full thrust power. Even if luck is with him the odds for a player surviving a season without a major injury are not too great. It takes every bit of coordination, awareness, acuteness, strength, ability and talent he possesses to maintain a superlative level of performance. Split-second timing and cool, clear-headed judgment are absolutely necessary at all times to stay on top of the heap and in control of the game. And if he doesn't, he knows there are several young men just waiting in the wings for his professional demise. In the past several years many athletes have resorted to amphetamines to operate at top-level skill, some with the consent, yes, even approval of management—*anything* to win the game or the pennant. Life (health) is cheap in the professional sports world; results are what count.

I had occasion to go to an acupuncture doctor in New York a few months ago. In the course of our conversation, he told me a story about an owner of one of the big pro football teams approaching him the week before to see if he would administer acupuncture to injured players to enable them to continue playing without pain, even at the eventual risk of permanent injury. Fortunately my doctor is a man of professional integrity. He warned the owner that to do so

Chart 20: **INCREASED SELF-ACTUALIZATION**

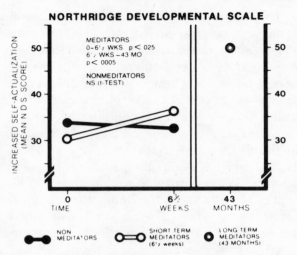

NORTHRIDGE DEVELOPMENTAL SCALE

INCREASED SELF-ACTUALIZATION (MEAN N D S SCORE)

MEDITATORS
0–6½ WKS p < 025
6½ WKS – 43 MO
p < 0005

NONMEDITATORS
NS (t-TEST)

50 — 50
40 — 40
30 — 30

0
TIME

6½
WEEKS

43
MONTHS

●━● NON MEDITATORS
○━○ SHORT TERM MEDITATORS (6½ weeks)
◎ LONG TERM MEDITATORS (43 MONTHS)

This test shows that the benefits of TM are cumulative.

Chart 21: **IMPROVED MENTAL HEALTH**

Clinical Application
MINNESOTA MULTIPHASIC PERSONALITY INVENTORY

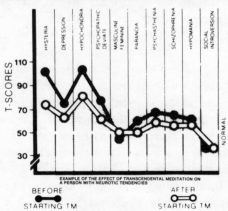

T-SCORES

110
90
70
50
30

HYSTERIA · DEPRESSION · HYPOCHONDRIA · PSYCHOPATHIC DEVIATE · MASCULINE FEMININE · PARANOIA · PSYCHASTHENIA · SCHIZOPHRENIA · HYPOMANIA · SOCIAL INTROVERSION

NORMAL

EXAMPLE OF THE EFFECT OF TRANSCENDENTAL MEDITATION ON
A PERSON WITH NEUROTIC TENDENCIES

●━● BEFORE STARTING TM

○━○ AFTER STARTING TM

Meditators are less apt to be hypochondriacs, schizophrenic, and show an overall improvement in mental health.

Chart 22: IMPROVED RESISTANCE TO DISEASE I

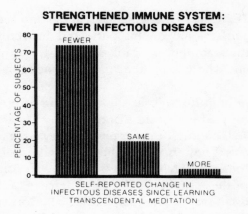

**STRENGTHENED IMMUNE SYSTEM:
FEWER INFECTIOUS DISEASES**

SELF-REPORTED CHANGE IN
INFECTIOUS DISEASES SINCE LEARNING
TRANSCENDENTAL MEDITATION

Chart 23: IMPROVED RESISTANCE TO DISEASE II

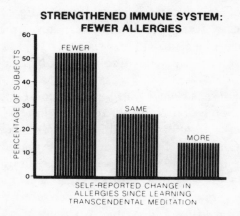

**STRENGTHENED IMMUNE SYSTEM:
FEWER ALLERGIES**

SELF-REPORTED CHANGE IN
ALLERGIES SINCE LEARNING
TRANSCENDENTAL MEDITATION

For the population in general, as I've discussed, TM has remarkable impact on the meditators body and soul. The following charts prove TM's potential in keeping the meditator healthy as well as in harmony. Aside from the obvious alleviation of pain and discomfort, the results shown here can save us all tremendous amounts in our medical bills.

would be extremely detrimental to the injured player, highly unprofessional on his part, and he refused. The owner of the team left in a huff, saying, "If you won't, I'll find someone who will for the kind of money I'm prepared to pay."

Naturally, it doesn't take a team long to be aware of what kind of s.o.b. they are working for. They soon know they have to look out for themselves if they want to survive as ball players. They also know that drugs take their physical toll in the long run. Therefore it is not too surprising to find not a few of these superstars into the practice of Transcendental Meditation: Joe Namath, Eddie Ball, Bob Svihus and Al Woodall of the New York Jets; Bill Walton, center, UCLA basketball team; Pete Broberg, pitcher, Texas Rangers; Bryant Salter, defensive back, San Diego Chargers; Craig Lincoln, Olympic Medal winner and diving coach at University of Minnesota; Chuck Walker, goalie, Dartmouth College hockey team; Bill Dunlap, captain, Amherst College ski team; Julia Tancock, professional figure skater; Pete Medley, former C.I.F. wrestling champion. And they are but a few.

These athletes report "surges" of natural energy from meditating. Some noted quicker reaction time; less tension; better concentration; more flexibility; better balance; easier breathing. One long distance runner said that after a few weeks of meditating he relaxed so much he thought he was getting lazy, not pushing hard enough. Yet after timing himself every day for a month he discovered his overall time was reduced by ten to fifteen percent.

One athlete put it in the vernacular of the day: "TM gives me the *edge* that all athletes need over their opponents."

As more and more athletes of stature are beginning to practice meditation, more and more coaches, managers and

Chart 24: **NORMALIZATION OF WEIGHT**

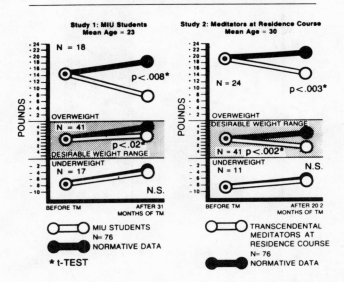

Look out Dr. Atkins! TM may steal your stuff.

owners are becoming increasingly aware of these concrete benefits, and major league teams are showing interest in having TM taught to their entire lineups. (Estimates for original teaching and follow-up TM to a major league base-ball team runs somewhere in the neighborhood of $4,500 for a seven-month program.) It should prove extremely interesting to see what effects the program will have on their performance as a whole. If appreciable results are shown by the performance of these teams next season, if indeed it does give an entire team that sought after "edge" over the competition, it could well change the entire physi-ological concept of professional sports.

Chart 25: **SUPERIOR PERCEPTUAL-MOTOR PERFORMANCE**

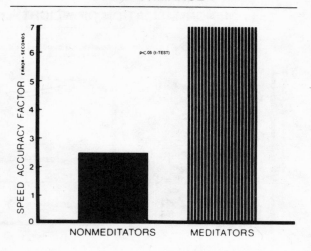

Chart 26: **FASTER REACTION TIME**

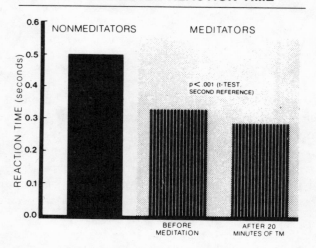

Not only are the results of these studies interesting to athletes, but laborers who work with their hands and the armed forces should also take note.

Chart 27: **IMPROVED ATHLETIC PERFORMANCE**

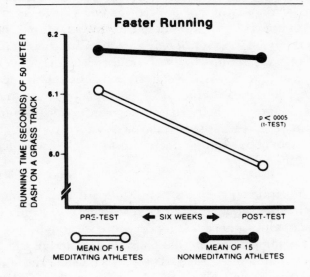

Faster Running

RUNNING TIME (SECONDS) OF 50 METER DASH ON A GRASS TRACK

6.2

6.1

6.0

$p < 0005$
(t-TEST)

PRE-TEST ← SIX WEEKS → POST-TEST

○━○ MEAN OF 15 MEDITATING ATHLETES

●━● MEAN OF 15 NONMEDITATING ATHLETES

Coaches (and cowards), look at these fantastic results after just six weeks of TM!

I recently spoke with the head of the Institute for Fitness and Athletics, and he informed me that the Philadelphia Phillies, i.e., nine players, the owner, general manager, three administrators and two of the wives had signed up for TM.

While I had the director, Don Leopold, on the phone I said to him, "That's exciting news. Let me ask you something. What do you think was the significant thing that sold the Phillies on the idea of TM. What one thing in particular do you think convinced them, *en masse,* to try it?"

"That's easy," he said. "Endurance. Endurance is a major factor in winning the ball game. The team whose strength holds out for the whole game is bound to come up a winner in the long run. Their schedules are so tight in the heart of the season, what with double headers, traveling, change in time across the country, anxieties about performance, about the other team . . . it's the guys who can hold up the longest at their peak performance who eventually win out. That's what sold them! The actual proof I could show them about getting deeper rest I think is what finally turned the trick."

The following charts, which record the findings of more than ten different sets of researchers, certainly indicate enough evidence to support more thorough, intricate and ongoing studies into the physiological and psychological effects of TM. Science has barely scratched the surface of the various benefits that TM has for the human body.

Since the cranium is connected to the torso and they must live together in harmony or perish, I must agree with George Bernard Shaw when he said, "A sound mind in a sound body is a stupid saying—a sound body is the product of a sound mind."

SEX AND LOVE

11

> *"If you cultivate within yourself a natural state
> of kindness, compassion, love and forgiveness,
> you will receive a thousandfold reward from the
> surroundings.*
>
> MAHARISHI MAHESH YOGI

SEX and love; love and sex? Which comes first, the chicken or the egg, the tree or the seed?

When I was growing up in a little college town in the Pennsylvania hinterlands, I can't remember the word SEX being mentioned aloud in proper homes or gatherings. Clark Gable and Carole Lombard in their raciest movies never, *ever* entered the boudoir without having first gone through the great knot-tying, double-ring ceremony. Even in a crazy mixed-up farce where the leading lady found herself inextricably stranded by some curious twist of fate in a bachelor's quarters, he *always* gave up his bedroom *and* his oversize pajamas to the damsel in distress while he, like the perfect gentleman, ended up fully clothed, pretzel-fashion, uncomfortably balanced all night long between

155

two living room chairs. God and the Hayes censor office had forbidden otherwise. There were no complicated initials on the marquees or in the advertising deciding who could see the movie and who couldn't. Movies were for the entire family.

Today they show films that must have our grandparents spinning out of their graves straight into orbit. Today you don't have to sneak into your father's study while he's at the office and look into the family medical volumes to see what IT looks like, or how to do IT.

The advent of "The Pill" has unleashed a force just slightly inferior in strength to the splitting of the atom: womanpower. In the old days we thought it was good, old-fashioned Christian morals that kept Little Nell from the Primrose Path. But alas, the invention of the pill has blown that theory into orbit along with our dead grandparents, and sent your average, insecure, redblooded American male scurrying to the nearest shrink because he either can't get it up or can't keep it up. The pill that was to liberate the female has turned into an emasculating monster for Big Daddy. For that reason alone marriages in this country are breaking up faster than Pompeii in its final hours.

The contemporary counterparts of our mothers, who whiled away many an afternoon hanging over the back fence and gossiping with each other while the sheets were drying, are now slipping between those very sheets with each other, while the kids are off to an X-rated movie and Big Daddy is paying somebody else's daughter a hundred bucks for a half hour's time to reassure himself of his manhood. Homosexuals are openly declaring themselves, fighting for their rights—and their love nest at the chic, restricted Riverhouse Apartments.

The moral temples of yesteryear have been desecrated.

Unisex is the odds-on favorite for the next presidential election. Sexual anarchy and chaos prevail. All this has happened in the short span of a quarter of a century. We had all better sharpen our streaking shoes if we hope to keep up with the *next* twenty-five years.

One of two favorite poems which my father loved to recite was Kipling's *If.* (The other was *I Learned about Women from Her!*) *If* goes something like this: "If you can keep your head while all about you others are losing theirs . . ."

That was one of his simple credos for living a good, happy life. And I have found over the years that it has stood me in pretty good stead (when I can keep my head long enough to remember it). What I'm trying to get at is *change* is the only thing that is constant, and the only way to deal with the mind-boggling speed of our changing world is to reach some sort of inner security. The other mainstay that my father was forever quoting to us kids when we went to him with our serious emotional problems was: "Know Thyself." He was long gone before I began to really understand what he was trying to convey with those two simple words.

Today both women and men's attitudes about each other have changed. Women no longer fall for the super aggressive male-wolf call. The American wolf is, practically speaking, an endangered species. The woman of today wants a sensitive man, both sexually and emotionally, with whom to live her life and raise her children; a husband who will share the responsibilities of raising the family and keeping the home; a man who recognizes her as an intellectual equal with equal rights and privileges—not just some vessel at his disposal in which to place his sperm when he so desires, carry his progeny until term and then rear it in his image. Today's woman is fighting for and getting the right to share in the sexual pleasures of marriage, including where, when and how; and also the right to decide if she wants to bear a child after it has been conceived. Much of the reason for the anger and hatred that have sometimes stemmed from the more radical women's liberationists is because these rights were too long in coming. The longer it takes for a revolution to begin, the bloodier it is. The very definition of revolution is radical change. It has taken since the history of mankind began until now for many of these changes to become effective. Yes, many an innocent man is going to suffer and many man*hoods* are going to perish before peace reigns between the sexes. Both sexes are going to have to learn to reevaluate themselves. Every man and every woman is going to have to look inward and learn to love themselves, to become aware of themselves and their true worth in the universal sense. They will have to learn that, unless they are happy with themselves, they will never be able to give happiness to their loved ones because they won't have any to give.

The young man of today also wants a different kind of spouse than his grandfather married. He saw his father either die in a war or live to return, build a business and a home, and raise a family. He was a father who had too little time to spend with his children when they were growing up and needed him, a father who was so laden with the financial and emotional responsibilities of giving his family "the good life" that he lost the whole purpose of it all. No, today's young man is beginning to realize that the sooner he liberates the women the sooner he himself will be liberated. Freedom begets freedom. What took us so long to learn that?

How many lovers do we know who wound up hating each other? Sit in a divorce court for a few sessions and listen to husbands and wives reviling each other, fighting over their chattels and children worse than wild beasts over

their territory. Most of these people were once lovers.
What happened? Where and how did it all go wrong?

I can only speak for my own great loves. It happened
bit by bit, inch by inch. Passion waltzed into love; love
changed to indifference; indifference twisted into jealousy;
and jealousy slipped into hate. All of us consider ourselves
reasonably intelligent people. Why can't we see it happening and do something about it, and why can't all those other
people whose beautiful, loving marriages disintegrate into
cesspools of misery for both of them? I think it is because
we don't know ourselves.

Through my meditation I am slowly but surely becoming aware of several hang-ups in myself that must have
contributed severely to the breakup of my own love affairs.
Some of them are the very same hang-ups that I defended
so stoutly when brought to task by my lovers. They are too
personal in nature to go into here, and besides, it's too late
now. Too much has passed between us ever to recoup our
great loss. But at least maybe next time I get lucky I won't
make the same mistakes—or will I?

Unless they invent another kind of pill, the kind that
gives eternal life, I can reasonably assume that my life is
two-thirds over, actuarily speaking. I have "loved" several
people in varying degress. I have been deeply, seriously in
love three times in my life. I've had many affairs, some of
which I entered into with the hope that something big
would come of it, a lasting and deep love. Except for the
three times I mentioned, they didn't work out that way. No
one's fault in particular, mostly the blame lay in a general
incompatibility. We wanted different things, different life
styles. They drank too much or I drank too much. The
timing was wrong. I was involved with my work and they
were out of a job. Vice versa. Their breath was bad. My
breath was bad. Whatever the reasons, they didn't pan out.

Some lasted a few weeks, some a few years. A few years not because we were too much in love to part but simply from inertia. It was too much trouble to break it off until one of us met someone more interesting.

I'm one of those people who really doesn't feel alive, complete, unless I'm in love. Everything else is secondary in my life. I like to consider myself a cerebral person, but I know that no matter how much I intellectualize a situation my final action is based on my emotions. I have turned away great amounts of money for love. I have turned away from my friends for love. I have let my work suffer for love. As sure as there's order in the universe and a God in the heavens, those three people loved me as deeply as I loved them—but we blew it!

I was very impressed by an article in *Newsweek* by author Willie Morris. In the article he says,

> In those inevitable moments of despoiling ill temper, as we damage what we cherish, we know that we can go elsewhere and soon. All the time we may have thought we were growing from the sinews of our own past experiences—for what is intelligence if not coping with the recurrences of one's existence?—learning somehow to give more of ourselves and to expect less, until one day we awaken in a cold dawn to see there are turbulent things in ourselves and those we love that we did not really comprehend at all, and that we are unable to conduct ourselves compassionately.

Deep love does involve deep compassion. We all have it somewhere in our depths. We simply have to find it or we are denying ourselves the greatest height that mankind can attain: love.

☐ David Aronson is a twenty-eight-year-old graduate student at Columbia University working on his thesis for his doctorate in law. He is an exceptionally good-looking young man with a decidedly higher-than-average I.Q. and education. David is from a well-to-do Jewish family whose mother is still alive and well in Great Neck, Long Island. His father was the president of a large textile company in New York City. He keeled over dead from a massive coronary after a tennis match a few years ago at the age of fifty-four, in perfect health according to the insurance doctor who passed him with flying colors six months previously. Post mortem diagnosis: "Too much work!"

David has now been practicing TM for approximately two years. Four years ago David met a nice Jewish girl with whom he fell in love and wanted to marry. Joan was studying law at Columbia University. She is beautiful, intelligent, sensitive and rich. They had the blessings of both their families and several months before the marriage was to take place they started sleeping together, as is the usual course of events in this day and age. And I for one think it is the greatest step forward that these young people have instituted in their upheaval of the old standards, possibly thanks to the pill. I can remember when I was in school, if a girl got pregnant she either had to leave school in disgrace, commit suicide, chance a highly dangerous illegal abortion *if* she could afford it, or marry the son of a bitch who knocked her up, as the expression went, whether they loved each other or not. Usually, though the boy felt he had been entrapped, he behaved like a gentleman and went ahead with the marriage, prematurely saddling himself with the added responsibility of two extra mouths to feed years before he was prepared, either financially or emotionally, to assume the added burden.

Well, what happened? In David's own unabashed words: "I blew it. I blew it sexually. I goofed."

His sexual life up to that time had been the usual

one-night stands with pickups from singles bars or casual encounters with girls from school. What did he know of the finer art of lovemaking? As his ardor with his fiancée increased, hers decreased until one day she called the whole thing off by simply stating over a gin and tonic at Mike Malkan's Bar, "It's no good, David. It's not going to work." He naturally tried to pin her down to more specific reasons but she would only say, "We're just not right for each other."

A year or so later they met one night at a party. Again he pursued it. She finally said, "All right, David, you asked for it. I'm going to level with you. You treated me like a piece of meat in bed. You didn't make love to me, you balled me, you screwed me, you fucked me but you *never* made love to me. For me, for the most part, it was terribly unrewarding and I couldn't see spending the rest of my life with some man who didn't know or didn't care enough to find out the difference . . . to think of *me,* of my pleasure, not just himself." He still didn't understand what she meant exactly but that was as specific as she cared to be. Shortly after that she married another law student and today is a happy wife, a proud mother of three, and a practicing lawyer.

David says today, hitting his head with the heel of his hand in exasperation at his own stupidity, "Finally, *finally* I know what she meant. . . ."

I said, "What *did* she mean? Explain to me, how did you find out, finally . . . ?"

"Well," he said, "I'll try. It's not easy, it goes back a couple of years now. I attended an introductory lecture in TM that was being held on campus one day. I got interested because some of my friends had told me about it and thought that it had helped them immeasurably with their studies, so I got into it. I can't be exactly sure when I began to notice the difference in myself but it was sometime after about a year of TM when I started seeing another girl fairly regularly. I began to notice up-front that our relationship, particularly in bed, was a lot different than it had been with Joan.

"I guess my whole attitude about people in general, not just girls, had changed. Slowly and imperceptibly but surely it changed. I began to look at people in a different light and of course women *are* people. Before that I guess I had thought of them, not as people, but just as girls—the ones I wanted to go to bed with and the ones I didn't. That was about the only distinguishing characteristic. It sounds terrible I know, but a lot of young guys feel that way, at least a lot of guys I know."

"How do you mean, 'particularly in bed' was different?" I asked.

All of a sudden, instead of a self-assured, cool, young legal eagle in front of me, I was facing an embarrassed, crimsoning boy. He searched for the proper words.

Being a woman practically old enough to be his mother *and* an interviewer made answering my question about as pleasant for him as the extraction of an impacted wisdom tooth at the turn of the century. We verbally fenced around a bit and after a good deal of parrying and thrusting he finally blurted out, "OK, you asked for it. I used to come, I mean ejaculate, almost immediately when I was in bed with Joan or, for that matter, any other girl. There was nothing I could do about it. It just happened. Nor did I care. That was the name of the game for me, getting it off. Now it's different. I mean my attitude about them is different. I look at them and feel about them as humans. The game is not to get off as quickly as possible but to extend myself emotionally to them as well as physically. I guess what I'm trying to say is *I touch them now,* and by touching them now I can *feel* them. Instead of getting instantly *hot,* I can feel myself gradually warming to them and they to me, and our warmth builds together and it's beautiful; and afterwards the feeling, that glow that holds over, is good. I guess I had never known what 'afterglow' meant. I know now, not only with a steady girl but even in casual affairs, that neither of us feel used or diminished afterwards but fuller and nicer inside.

"To be perfectly honest, I have since given a good deal of thought to my sex life with Joan. I have to admit that I guess I was scared I couldn't perform or I wouldn't be able to so I rushed everything just to get it over with.

"Since I have been meditating for almost a year I don't seem to have the fears, the anxieties I used to have, not only about sex but other areas as well. I was always a good student but before taking tests I used to get terribly anxious, not about flunking—I was too good for that—but I always set such high goals for my studies that I lived in fear I wouldn't live up to my ideas of myself. It's really just another kind of 'performance' fear. Those fears no longer exist. They seem to have dissipated. As a result, my grades are actually higher than they ever were and I don't study any longer or harder than I used to, and I'm a better lover, too. Explain that, if you can. I just feel better about being ME, not what I think other people think of me."

And then he wrapped it up: a kind of faraway nostalgic look came in his eyes and he said quietly, "I guess that was what Joan meant when she said I balled her but I never made love to her. . . ."

As you will have noted in the preceding chapters, I have tried, wherever possible, to back up the subjective claims presented by the teachers and the meditators' case histories with hard scientific test data regarding the specific subjects involved.

However, when I got to this chapter and looked over all the research data that I have compiled it was difficult because practically everything applies to our love lives. I mean, if you're tired, you don't feel like it. If you're anxious, you can't put your mind to it. If you're generally overwrought, the gentlest, most loving person can turn into an irritable, cranky monster. If you're worried about your health, your heart, your blood pressure, you might hesitate about having a really torrid sexual life. If you have been relying on alcohol or amphetamines to keep going, it undoubtedly hasn't improved your sex life; in fact, both of these generally make for impotence, if not incompetence.

Conversely, if you feel rested, relaxed, content with your personal performance in both your work and home life, nonanxious, stable, alert, able to cope and deal on a competent level with your daily life, and full of the old *joie de vivre,* it's bound to make a difference in the libidinous and loving areas of your lives. Statistically, healthy, happy people maintain a healthy sex/love life well into their eighties and sometimes, as some Russians in the Caucasian Mountains report, well into their hundred and twenties.

Therefore, the statistical data I have shown in the other chapters all, more or less, can be related to this area of our lives.

RELATING TO OTHERS

12

*The bamboo shadows are sweeping the stairs
But no dust is stirred.
The moonlight penetrates the depths of the pool,
But no trace is left in the water.*
from *BUDDHISM AND ZEN*

SOMETIMES it seems an almost impossible task to describe the experience of meditation and make it understandable in Western terms to our practical Western minds. The experience seems as elusive as the "bamboo shadows," at least when trying to capture it in words. And even though perhaps I should be the last person in the world to write this particular chapter, I think it is easier to understand what happens after learning and practicing the technique of meditation by putting my own experiences on the line.

Over the years I have been called, not just by people who didn't particularly care for me but occasionally by my friends, a variety of not too pleasant adjectives like cold, intolerant, uncompassionate, self-centered, bigoted, selfish, fascistic, ill-tempered, abrupt, insensitive, conceited and even cruel—a thoroughly ornery critter. And from time to time I'm sure they were right. But over the years I have learned, too often the hard way, that those attitudes in me simply didn't work. Through the examples of other people and the temperance of age, I have mellowed somewhat.

I was a spoiled brat and allowed to get away with too much by my brother and father, with whom I lived. I guess it had something to do with being the only female in the house. Whatever the reasons, the fact remains it made life very difficult for me when I finally left home and had to fend for myself in the great big world. If people didn't agree with me, I thought they were either stupid or crazy. If they criticized me, I became defensive. If they put me down, it made me snarky. I reacted badly to anything that didn't smack of absolute love and devotion. If they weren't *for* me, they were *against* me. Rules were made for other people to follow and me to break—with no penalties, of course. The community in which I lived was small. My family was among the privileged. I had uncles and aunts on the board of every bank and school in the town and an uncle who was one of the best all-around lawyers in the state. Nothing really bad could happen to me, no matter what deviltry I did.

Well, it didn't take me long to find out, once I had ceased to be a big fish in a little pond and struck out for the big pond of New York, that those halcyon days were over. The Big Apple had not only not heard of me but they hadn't even heard of my home town or my aunts and uncles!

I must not have been all bad because I was fortunate enough to gather about me some marvelous friends who helped me and stuck by me through the terribly difficult transitional periods, friends who put up with my peccadillos and taught me some of the hard facts of life. Pragmatist that I am, through their fine examples in dealing with life and work and other people, I had to admit to the simple fact that their way worked and mine didn't. Gradually I began to change my ways and my attitude about life in general and people in particular.

Even so, I was a hard nut to crack, but through the patience and understanding of some terrific employers, colleagues, friends and doctors I began to see the light. I began to learn things about myself. A lot of my defensiveness stemmed from my shyness and insecurities. As these things slowly began to melt away due to my efforts and accomplishments, I gained inner strength. As that strength grew so did my capacity to understand others. It didn't happen overnight. It took years for me to get to the point of not yelling back at rude taxi drivers, to the point where I could smile at perfect strangers, to the point of not having to get drunk *before* I went to a party so I could relax among strangers.

Socrates said, "The unexamined life is not worth living." I have to agree with him. Once *my* life got to the point where it wasn't worth living, simply because I had been doing things wrong, dealing with people wrong. I went to an analyst. It hurt and it helped. It hurt because it made me admit that I had been doing things wrong. It helped because, once I admitted these wrongs to myself and stopped blaming the rest of the world for my misery, I could begin to change.

We all know some miserable people, people who get out of bed in the morning feeling miserable and spread that misery to whomever they come in contact with until they go to bed that night. In a big city I think one is more aware of it, if for no other reason than that you come in contact with more strangers in a given period than a small community where everyone knows you. Strangers tend to mistrust each other unless they are outgoing people by nature. Recall your mother's last words before you left the house, "And remember, don't talk to strangers." With all motherly good intentions they instilled in us from childhood a basic distrust of strangers.

Most happy people are outgoing, giving human beings, helpful and generous of heart and purse. They can afford it because it gives them joy. It shows on their faces, in their homes and their children. Look around you. Think of the people you consider happy—or miserable. Observe the countenances of strangers. Their faces usually reflect their emotional state, particularly in repose. What kind of face do those strangers see when they observe you?

> "This day will not come again.
> Each minute is worth a priceless gem."
> *Taku-an*

And then there are those of us that fall into the in-between category: neither happy nor miserable. I had occasion not long ago to visit an old man I know. Old? He's seventy-two years *young.* A handsome, wise gentleman of the theater, a very successful character actor whom you have seen in many a soap opera and Broadway show. He is retired with his second wife and is writing his memoirs in Spain. A young German girl, also a friend of his, went with me. In the course of the conversation she said, "Geoffrey, you've lived a long time and done a lot with your life. Are you happy?"

He looked at her for a moment. A smile spread slowly across his beautiful face. In his mellifluous, cultured voice, he said, "Rita, I want to tell you something. This is nineteen hundred and seventy-three. I have, for all intents and purposes, had a good life. I have beautiful, healthy, loving children. I have a wonderful wife who loves me dearly or she'd never have put up with this old ham for so many years. I have my health and enough money to last me out."

He ruminated a bit more before he continued. "You asked me if I'm happy. My answer is, once, in nineteen hundred and thirty-six, I was sitting on a hilltop in the Adirondacks with a lovely young lady. It was a magnificent day, we had taken a picnic lunch with us. She was a charming companion. I was "between" wives, so to speak. My career was going swimmingly. The weather was glorious. I looked out at the sun shining on the mountain tops, took a deep breath of sweet, fresh air and said out loud to the world at large, "I'm happy. *Right now I'm happy!*" He raised his great white shaggy eyebrows, spread his arms wide with his hands palms-up and said, "That is the first and last time I have ever been happy and *known it.* I knew at *that* moment on *that* mountain top with *that* pretty young woman that *I was happy.* The rest of the time I've had too many responsibilities, too many worries about raising my family and furthering my career to ever be *there* again."

I'll remember that dear man saying that for the rest of my life. For weeks after I couldn't get it out of my thoughts. Is that what it's all about? Is that what a lifetime is all about? *Once,* in nineteen thirty-six? No, it can't be. Then I began to think about my life. How long had it been since I could remember catching a moment in time and space and saying out loud, "I'm happy, here and now!" I had to go back to 1959. That's f-i-f-t-e-e-n years ago.

I haven't been unhappy, but happy???

Shortly after that episode I started thinking about what I could do about my "contentedness," a word I use to denote a state of not-being-happy but not-being *un*happy— a sort of emotional netherland. That was about the same time I heard about TM and decided to look into it. I knew

I didn't want to get to be Geoffrey's age and have to answer that question as he had.

I know that TM is making me more aware of myself and my relation to my very BEING, my here and now BEING. I am beginning to care if days "slip" by, weeks "slip" by that are meaningless, humdrum; and I am beginning to do something about it to make them more meaningful. This axiomatically carries over in my relationship with other people. I want to make contact with them and have them make contact with me. I want to feel the impact of daily living, to tactilely experience the fleeting moments. We can only do this by expanding our awareness of life and the living creatures and things that we deal with from day to day, nay, minute to minute.

The karma we can spread by smiling at people, the good will that grows from just taking that extra second to be interested enough to ask about another person's life and welfare: try telling the next taxi driver you hire what a good driver he is and see the results. L-o-o-k at the next person you meet at a party, pick out something about him that is pleasing and tell him about it. Notice his reaction.

My analyst, God rest her soul, was an old German woman with a face like Santa Claus. The only words I can recall her saying to me in the two years I went to her were, "You show your darkness to the world and keep the light inside you. Let your light shine out. That is where your happiness lies. . . ."

Maharishi Mahesh Yogi says, "If one is not happy one has lost the very purpose of life." He says, "Life is not meant to be lived in dullness, idleness and suffering."

I can't remember to what school of psychoanalysis my old German lady belonged, but I am sure it wasn't the same one Maharishi went to, and yet in essence they are both saying the same thing. My grandfather was a Presbyterian minister. He preached more or less the same words from his pulpit.

Where did we go wrong? At what point did we get off the track? To refer to the quote that headed this chapter: Did we stop cultivating? Did we stop giving? Or both?

Maharishi says, "The first fundamental in the art of behavior is: meet with warmth and meet to give. If all people in society behaved on this level of giving, social behavior could only result in the advancement and glorification of everyone's life."

According to Christopher Isherwood in his *Vedanta for the Western World,* Karma means action, work, deed. Not only physical action, conscious or reflex, but also mental action, conscious or subconscious. Karma is everything that we think or do. Philosophically speaking, Karma also means the Law of Causation: a law which is said to operate in the physical, mental and moral spheres of our lives.

I do an action; I think a thought. The Vedantist tells me that this action and this thought, even though they are apparently over and done with, will inevitably, sooner or later, produce some effect. This effect may be pleasant, unpleasant, or a mixture of both. It may be long delayed. I may never notice it. I may have altogether forgotten the action or the thought which caused it. Nevertheless, it will be produced.

Furthermore, every action and every thought makes an impression upon the mind. This impression may be slight at first, but if the same action or thought is repeated, it will deepen into a kind of groove down which our future behavior will easily tend to run. These mental grooves we call our tendencies. Their existence makes it possible to predict fairly accurately just how each of us will behave in any given situation. In other words, *the sum of our Karma represents our character.* We cut ourselves off from so much pleasure by not pleasing others, by not extending ourselves more. The pebble of pleasure we skip across a pond causes just as many ripples as the pebble of pain. Try it, what have you got to lose?

One has to start dealing with others very early in life. Forgetting about the different intricacies of dealing with one's own parents, brothers and sisters, we really start out on our own coping with our peer groups. No matter how much you get away with at home, the second you start associating with kids your own age life changes drastically. I imagine for an only child life is doubly difficult.

First we must learn to share: our candy, our toys, our ideas, and we see that our friends have to share with us. We learn rapidly at that age that it is a give and take proposition that works. If we don't adjust to that fact quickly we find we are unpopular.

The first time that I can remember being brought up short was by my brother who was three and a half years older than I. I'd had a terrible argument with some of my little baseball playmates about who was playing first base. I stomped home in an indignant rage and I screamed to my brother, "I hate them, I hate them. I'll never speak to them again." A twinkle crept into his eyes as he said, "Boy, you'll fix them, won't you, kiddo?" It was then that I realized that the game goes on, with or without me.

Perhaps the most painful thing in life is to lose a friend of long standing by a misunderstanding. It doesn't matter whose fault it is or where the blame lies, both parties suffer. Pride is usually the factor that keeps misunderstanding alive. Someone has to make the first move for the reconciliation. The longer it takes, the more difficult it gets. How many times do we cut off our nose to spite our face, as the old saying goes? In high school we used to say, "Get wise to yourself."

Maharishi says, "Angry words pollute the environment." The Bible says, "Do unto others as you would have them do unto you." I say, "The next time you're full of anger and hate and uptightness, look in the mirror and see what it does to your face!"

In the final analysis we must first learn to deal with ourselves. Meditating helps us achieve this state of calmness that is required to handle the gratuitous hostilities that surround our daily existence so that we don't find it necessary to fight fire with fire, negativism with negativism—otherwise mankind really is going to die with a whimper, snuffed out of existence in a billowing cloud of hot air.

We all want to make sure that the poet Samuel Hoffenstein wasn't referring to us in his great one-liner wrapup: "Wherever I go, I go too and spoil everything."

Since I have been meditating I really have begun to deal with people and situations-and-people differently—not all the time, but sometimes. For one thing, I find myself *trying* to be kinder, more thoughtful of other's feelings, more conscious of what effect my actions and deeds will have on them (and eventually me).

We all use people, as we use things, to satisfy our needs and fulfill our desires. There is nothing wrong with using people. Where we get into trouble is when we *misuse* people. I am beginning to realize when and how I was misusing my friends and everyday acquaintances. It was mostly by doing little inconsiderate things that were so small they didn't bother to mention them, or by ignoring things that used to be called "common courtesies"—that in this swiftly paced day and age seem, for the most part, to have gone by the boards. Sometimes it was something as simple as not remembering to call and thank someone for dinner and taking practically everything anyone did for me for granted, as my due. Oh, eventually I knew I would get around to reciprocating, unless of course I didn't. Needless to say, over the years one can run through an extraordinary number of people by dealing with them in such a high handed and cavalier manner. In the past few months I find myself taking better care of my friends, thinking more about *their* needs and desires as well as my own.

I'm not sure I can attribute it all to TM but it sure hasn't hurt. It stands to reason that if you aren't coiled up like a tight spring all the time, you aren't as likely to strike like a cobra whenever things don't go exactly as you had planned them. Meditating has, for one thing, uncoiled my tight springs a lot and, as a consequence, benefited my relationships with other people. I'm simply not as nervous as I used to be.

Another interesting manifestation is that I tend to be seeing people and their particular emotional difficulties more holistically. By that I mean I don't collapse in a heap of bitter disillusionment when my friends do something that changes my image of them somewhat or when they disappoint me for some small reason or other. I am beginning to realize that I have to accept them as a whole package as they have to accept me. In other words, I expect them to put up with my imperfections and I must put up with theirs. I somehow feel more mature in my relationships with them. Whereas I used to clam up and not speak to them for months on end if they did something that offended my sense of justice (toward me), now I speak up and tell them what I think they did wrong, and we talk it out like adults who are honestly trying to communicate and understand one another. This in itself relieves much anxiety. And I have found that, as stress builds stress and tension begets tension, de-stressing conversely tends to de-stress in a beneficial circle as opposed to a vicious circle.

The same goes for difficult situations. I now seem to be

Chart 28: **INCREASED NORMALITY**

NETHERLANDS PERSONALITY INVENTORY

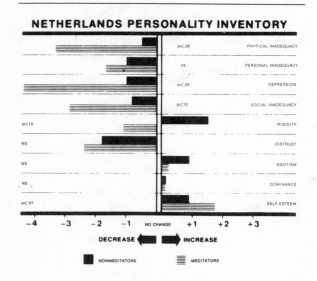

We might well be the life of the next party if TM has the same results on us that it did on the group tested above before and after TM.

able to see them as a whole and to be able to salvage what is salvageable instead of saying to hell with it and throwing out the baby with the bath water when things get rough. That has saved me time, effort, money and friends.

Since the practice of TM lessens anxieties, helps to achieve self-actualization and reduce irritability, it is not difficult to see how this could carry over into your dealings with other people: friends, spouse, lovers, all your family, co-workers, superiors—everybody! It could make life a lot more pleasant all the way around.

LEARNING

13

Man's life is to cultivate and give, cultivate the
divine power, the divine intelligence, happiness
and abundance and give it out to all of
creation.

MAHARISHI MAHESH YOGI

Knowledge cannot be obtained without effort—a
fact which is fairly generally accepted. But the
ludicrous methods which are used to project
effort, and the absurdity of the efforts themselves,
effectively close the gateway to knowledge for
people who try to transfer the learning systems of
one field to that of another.

THE SUFIS

A SMALL child's brain is like a computer, a virginal
memory bank, a sponge that indiscriminately soaks up
and stores everything and anything that is fed into it in
those extremely formative early years. In the beginning
days of the computer there was a sort of joke that traveled
around the business world describing the possible disadvan-

177

tages of using computers. It consisted of four letters—GIGO—meaning garbage in, garbage out! It is the same thing with a child's mind. It all depends on what is fed into it and how the child is taught to apply that knowledge in living terms that will determine what values the child will have and live by.

I have found, looking back on my own education and that of many friends, that all too often the method used was the endless repetition of information in a worn-out pattern of boring memorization of facts and figures that held no lasting meaning of any kind for the student. Once in a great while we were fortunate enough to come across a dynamic teacher who invested the material with his or her own vision of life, and that teacher never failed to find a hungry audience that was all-too-ready to learn on a deeper level.

In my reading of Maharishi and the Sufis and others, again and again I have found corroboration of my own experience with "education." "Many schools continue to operate long after their actual dynamic is exhausted, becoming mere centers repeating a progressively weakened doctrine. The name of the teaching may remain the same. The teaching may have no value, may even oppose the original meaning, is almost always a travesty of it." So say the Sufis. And, "Because the average person thinks in patterns and cannot accommodate himself to a really different point of view, he loses a great deal of the meaning of life. He may live, even progress, but he cannot understand all that is going on." Further, "Internal experience cannot be transmitted through repetitiousness, but has to be constantly refreshed at the source."

I agree with Robert Ornstein when he says that formal "education consists predominantly of readin', ritin' and 'rithmetic, and we are taught precious little about our emotions, our bodies, our intuitive capabilities." In the travels and research interviews I have conducted in connection with TM and this book I have had occasion to speak with many students, post graduates and teachers. Many of them told me that they had at one point in their scholastic pursuits dropped out of school because they couldn't quite get together the formal education they were receiving with the purpose of their lives. Their education seemed to be at cross-purposes or an isolated experience in their lives instead of *smoothly molding* into a fuller existence. More than one of them used the word "fragmented" in defining their college experience. In essence they were all more or less concurring that what was missing in the educational concept was a holistic approach. They, as students, began to feel departmentalized. Although they may have graduated as specialists in a particular field, they expressed a feeling of unpreparedness if they by some chance happened out of their own bailiwick. Many of them, even in their own fields, couldn't fit their knowledge into a universal scheme of things to a degree that made the entire effort seem worthwhile. They complained that many of the courses were taught without the very essence, the soul of the subject, ever being brought out.

This view gains even greater validity after the Watergate fiasco where so many bright, young, promising, dedicated attorneys, graduates from a multitude of different universities and socio-economic backgrounds, turned out to be, if not totally unscrupulous, then certainly lacking in moral and ethical character and judgment. What went wrong? These young men were not extraordinary villains. On the contrary, they seemed quite average. One thing about them all was the same; they all spent several years being educated in the legal profession and were all legally licensed "friends of the court" who had sworn under oath to uphold the laws of this country. Obviously those years in class and apprenticeship were spent in learning how to get around the law legally, not in learning about the soul of the law and their responsibility to uphold it and propagate by virtue of example the very letter and purpose of their profession, to see that justice prevails. Since Watergate there have been rumblings heard from various national and state bar associations and venerable deans of law in our more prestigious seats of learning about the necessity for changes to be made, but I seriously doubt there will be—anymore than the revelations of the Knapp Commission significantly changed the basic structure and morality of the New York Police Department.

Maharishi contends that the system will not change until man changes, and he is not alone in his contention. Most classical philosophers agree with him. Krishnamurti says, "We human beings, as individuals, are totally responsible for wars by the way we lead our lives." "When one realizes, not intellectually but actually, as actually as you would recognize that you are hungry, that you and I as human beings are responsible for all this chaos, for all this misery—because we contribute to it, we are part of it. . . ." He goes on to say that, "Only when we realize how serious this is, will we act on it." And again, "Not until you feel that you are completely responsible for this monstrous society, with its wars, with its divisions, with its ugliness, brutalities, greeds and so on, not until each one of us realizes this, will we act." This, in essence, is what Maharishi is trying to get across through his integrated educational program. No matter what subject you happen to be studying, everything, everyone and every action is interrelated.

Maharishi says: Let us not forget that every one of us is responsible for our national crisis. What is the cause of such a collective calamity? It is the collective tensions of the individuals. And what causes collective tensions? Individual tensions appearing as anger, fear, hatred, greed, jealousy, wrong thought, speech, action and corrupt practices of all sorts. Individual tensions accumulate in the atmosphere as collective tensions and produce collective calamities, national crises and international conflicts. Elimination of the existing tensions in the atmosphere is the urgent need of our time. Meeting the national crisis on its level is certainly necessary but a remedy to eliminate the existing tension in the atmosphere must be considered to be of equal importance, if not more. It is our national duty to alleviate the atmospheric tensions as soon as possible by eliminating the tensions in the lives of every individual. This can best be accomplished by a few minutes of daily practice of Transcendental Meditation.

On how many facades of our great institutes of learning, universities, libraries, museums is deeply inscribed in marble, "Know Thyself"? How many graduates solemnly leave those seats of knowledge carrying cum laude honors who are totally barren in knowledge of themselves and their responsibility to the world? Just in this country alone, how many Tea Pot Domes and Watergates will we have to suffer before we are shaken up, wakened up enough to change our educational system?

Maharishi established a university in Goleta, California called the Maharishi International University which has a recognized charter from the state of California. I feel the following excerpts from the Congressional Record introduced to the second session of the 93rd Congress by Senator Tunney can better express the goals and concepts of the SCI educational program than I.

The major question posed by educators and the public in relation to the process of higher education has been: What is the proper role of the institution of higher learning in society today? Maharishi International University provides a unique answer to this question—education is complete only when men and women everywhere are provided simultaneously with knowledge and the ability to use their full creative potential. MIU accomplished this by teaching the traditional academic disciplines along with the study of Science of Creative Intelligence.

The Science of Creative Intelligence is an interdisciplinary study, drawing upon the arts and sciences, which gives understanding of the nature, growth and development of creative intelligence in life. While MIU Offers to its students the full range of academic disciplines, the Science of Creative Intelligence reveals to the student the interrelationship of all knowledge as an expression of intelligence and creativity. In this way, academic understanding is never isolated from personal experience.

The practical aspect of this science is Transcendental Meditation (TM), a simple, natural, mechanical technique which enables students to experience directly and to develop the full range of this potential. The practical benefits of this technique have attracted the attention of scientists in the United States and Europe. Their research has demonstrated that Transcendental Meditation produces a unique state of the nervous system characterized by profound physical rest together with heightened mental alertness. This practice leads to greater mental and physical stability, efficiency and increased energy for purposeful activity. In addition, further studies have shown that practitioners of the technique exhibit a significant increase in intelligence and learning ability.

Further, the MIU education is not limited to walls of a single campus or the needs of a specific age group. MIU has designed programs that bring the advantages of higher education to all members of society, independent of the constraints of occupation or geographic location, economic situation or ethnic background. In addition to the main MIU campus in Goleta, California, MIU teaching centers in every major American city will present these courses through closed circuit color instructional television, and through the facilities of public broadcasting the value of the MIU education will soon be available to every home."

Maharishi International University was established in 1971 under the laws of the State of California as a nonprofit educational institution with teaching programs leading to the baccalaureate and doctoral degrees. The decision to establish Maharishi International University (MIU) arose directly from the enthusiasm of faculty, administration, students and parents at more than 600 college and university campuses in the United States who had witnessed the enlivening results of engaging in the practice of the Science of Creative Intelligence (SCI) as taught by Maharishi Mahesh Yogi. By the end of 1973 more than 300,000 Americans had participated in such programs with an additional 16,000 beginning each month.

The first credit-bearing course in the Science of Creative Intelligence was offered at Stanford University in 1970. Since then, similar accredited courses have been offered at more than thirty American universities, including Yale, Harvard and the University of California at Berkeley. The profound benefits of the knowledge and practice of the Science of Creative Intelligence and the validation of these benefits by physiological, psychological and sociological research conducted at leading universities and research institutes have provided a vision of possibility for the fulfillment of systems of education everywhere.

In the summer of 1971 the first Symposium on the Science of Creative Intelligence was held at the Amherst campus of the University of Massachusetts and was attended by internationally acclaimed research scientists, scholars and educators. These men and women, in response to the success of the symposium and the overwhelming national recognition of the Science of Creative Intelligence, determined to create a new university dedicated to the highest ideals of education and named to honor the founder of SCI, Maharishi Mahesh Yogi.

Maharishi International University feels that the contributions of its unique curriculum should not be limited to one geographic area but should be made available in all parts of the world. Therefore, the University has implemented a World Plan to establish 3,600 World Plan teaching centers internationally, one for each one million population to teach the Science of Creative Intelligence and to offer basic MIU courses for undergraduate and graduate degrees. Through this plan, MIU aims to accomplish the following seven goals:

(1) to develop the full potential of the individual;
(2) to improve governmental achievements;
(3) to realize the highest ideal of education;
(4) to eliminate age-old problems of crime and all behavior that brings unhappiness to the family of man;
(5) to maximize the intelligent use of the environment;
(6) to bring fulfillment to the economic aspirations of individuals and society; and
(7) to achieve the spiritual goals of mankind in this generation.

The motto of MIU is "Knowledge is structured in consciousness."

I quote an excerpt from Maharishi's inaugural address at the First International Symposium on the Science of Creative Intelligence at the University of Massachusetts in the summer of 1971:

Since the physical properties of phenomena differ, the study of the physical nature of things alone can never present a common basis for all knowledge. A common basis can only be found in something that is the same in all phenomena and in every study. Order in nature and man's power of ordering show that intelligence is at the core of every physical existence and every human mind. The study of the nature of intelligence, therefore, can be the common ground of all knowledge. Thus it is creative intelligence which is the dynamic of interdisciplinary study through which its goal can be achieved. Established on this foundation of all knowledge, everyone will feel at home in every field of investigation and achieve maximum efficiency in thought and action.

Students at the MIU express extraordinary excitement in the school's teaching methods. Many students switched to MIU from other major campuses across the country after getting into TM. Some are downright enthralled because for the first time in their college careers they are getting an overall view of the subject of study and how it relates to the nature of things. For instance, one drastic difference is that they take a ten-week course in ten different subjects. Instead of changing classes every hour or two they are thoroughly immersed in one subject for one entire week before moving on to the next the following week, thereby achieving much greater depth and concentration in that specific area of study.

They contend that this method of total immersion for one entire week makes the courses fascinating. Conceptually it makes sense: the more knowledge we have about something the more interesting it can be. What better way to achieve this than by total immersion, without interference. The ultimate goal for the graduate is self-actualization. In his lecture at the TM weekend retreat at Livingston Manor, Dr. Herbert Bloomfield quoted psychologist Abraham Maslow, describing the values of self-actualization as: wholeness, perfection, orderliness, spontaneity, richness, goodness, effortlessness, playfulness and self-sufficiency.

In paraphrasing Maharishi, Bloomfield said it was in the nature of an acorn to become a tall oak tree; similarly, it is in the nature of a human being to attain his highest potentiality or, in Eastern thought, achieve Cosmic Consciousness —*an inevitable unfolding process if we tap our creative intelligence.*

Jiddu Krishnamurti, the noted philosopher, says about education:

> It is the basic function of education to help you to find out what you really love to do, so that you can give your whole mind and heart to it, *because that creates human dignity, that sweeps away mediocrity,* the petite bourgeois mentality. That is why it is very important to have the right teachers, the right atmosphere, so that you will grow up with the love which expresses itself in what you are doing. Without this love your examinations, your knowledge, your capacities, your position and possessions are just ashes, they have no meaning; without this love your actions are going to bring more wars, more hatred, more mischief and destruction.

As noted in *Buddhism and Zen,* the Zen Buddhists, say:

> When one devotes himself to meditation, his mental burdens drop off, one by one; he feels that things go smoothly and somewhat pleasantly. A student may now depend on his intuition to make decisions. As he moves "at first glance," second thought with its dualism, doubt and hesitation, does not arise.

The following charts, reflecting studies of TM on the educational and intelligence processes, should be of particular interest to people working with retarded children and teachers and parents of students who have difficulty with their marks. Just by meditating your capacity of memory and learning can increase.

Chart 29: **INCREASED LEARNING ABILITY**

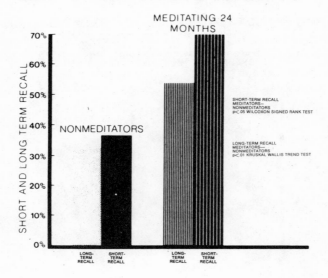

MEDITATING 24 MONTHS

NONMEDITATORS

SHORT AND LONG TERM RECALL

SHORT-TERM RECALL
MEDITATORS—
NONMEDITATORS
p< 05 WILCOXON SIGNED RANK TEST

LONG-TERM RECALL
MEDITATORS—
NONMEDITATORS
p< 01 KRUSKAL WALLIS TREND TEST

LONG-TERM RECALL SHORT-TERM RECALL LONG-TERM RECALL SHORT-TERM RECALL

Chart 30: **INCREASED INTELLIGENCE GROWTH RATE**

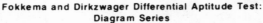

Fokkema and Dirkzwager Differential Aptitude Test: Diagram Series

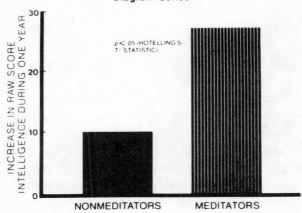

INCREASE IN RAW SCORE INTELLIGENCE DURING ONE YEAR

p< 05 (HOTELLING S T- STATISTIC)

NONMEDITATORS   MEDITATORS

Chart 31: **IMPROVED ACADEMIC PERFORMANCE**

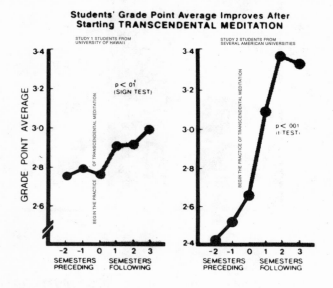

**Students' Grade Point Average Improves After
Starting TRANSCENDENTAL MEDITATION**

A great number of educational systems and administrators originally became interested in TM due to the early Benson and Wallace research which showed definite advances in the reduction of drug addiction among students.

Then there began to emerge a tremendous interest in the Science of Creative Intelligence as an entity in itself as raw data accumulated, became processed, filtered and refined into hard scientific results showing improved and expanded potentialities of meditators as opposed to nonmeditating students and academic instructors.

It has gained international recognition and financial support from several governments and international educational facilities:

In Ethiopia the Ministry of Education and Fine Arts "has given permission that SCI be taught in schools and colleges as a knowledge that is both useful and necessary to the progress of the individual."

In Denmark, SCI and TM are taught as part of the "evening school" program and are subsidized by city authorities and the Ministry of Education. The city government of Aarhus, Denmark, finances teachers of SCI to teach throughout the city.

In Sweden the civic governments of Malmo and Stockholm subsidize the teaching of TM and SCI through the Student's International Meditation Society by paying thirty percent of the center's rent and five krona per meditator per year.

In Delphi, Greece, on July 5, 1973, the municipal council presented to Maharishi the Golden Medal of the City of Delphi, *honoris causa*, because the goals of SCI, of which he is the founder, and of the technique of TM, which brings to light and actualizes all the latent potentialities of man, are "found to be synonymous with the ideal of the Delphic Amphictyons and the Delphic ordinances." (The Delphic Amphictyon was the ancient assembly of all Greek states which aimed at achieving the highest ideal of mankind.)

The United States Government Commissioner of Education gave the seal of approval to the MIU, thereby enabling it to apply for: grants for construction of undergraduate facilities; loans for construction of academic facilities; annual interest grants for construction of academic facilities; community service and continuing education; education opportunity grants (for undergrads only); insured student loans; cooperative education program; college work study; national direct student loans; improvement of undergraduate instruction and college library resources.

In 1972 the National Institute of Mental Health awarded

Chart 32: DEVELOPED PERSONALITY

MIU SANTA BARBARA CAMPUS
Results of Personality Testing

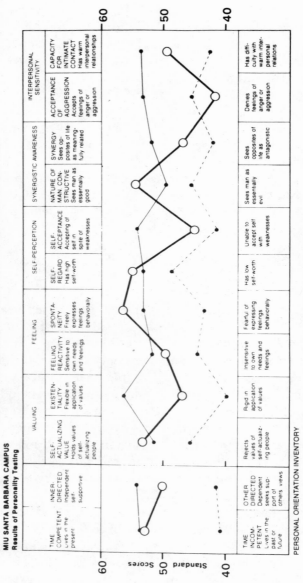

PERSONAL ORIENTATION INVENTORY

○—— Students entering MIU (N = 210) tested at the MIU Campus, Santa Barbara, scored consistently higher on scales of self-actualization than students entering other colleges and comparably in many respects to people judged as "self-actualizing."

●----● Normative data for students entering other colleges were based on 2,046 subjects.

●——● Normative data on persons clinically judged as "self-actualizing" were based on 29 subjects. All normative data were taken from the manual of Personal Orientation Inventory, Educational and Industrial Testing Service, U.S.A.

Reference David W. Orme-Johnson. Psychological Testing of MIU Students: First Report." *Scientific Research on Transcendental Meditation. Collected Papers Vol. 1*, ed. David W. Orme-Johnson.
Lawrence H. Domash and John T. Farrow (Los Angeles MIU Press, 1974).

Chart 33: DEVELOPED INTELLIGENCE

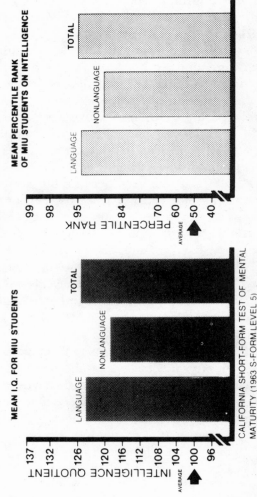

MIU SANTA BARBARA CAMPUS
Results of Intelligence Testing

MEAN I.Q. FOR MIU STUDENTS

MEAN PERCENTILE RANK
OF MIU STUDENTS ON INTELLIGENCE

LANGUAGE   NONLANGUAGE   TOTAL

INTELLIGENCE QUOTIENT

137
132
126
120
116
112
108
104
100 AVERAGE
96

PERCENTILE RANK

99
98
95
84
70
60
50 AVERAGE
40

CALIFORNIA SHORT-FORM TEST OF MENTAL
MATURITY (1963 S-FORM LEVEL 5)

A random sample of MIU students (N = 168) had a mean IQ of 125, which places them above 95% of the general population on intelligence.

Reference: David W. Orme-Johnson, "Psychological Testing of MIU Students: First Report," *Scientific Research on Transcendental Meditation: Collected Papers Vol. 1*, ed. David W. Orme-Johnson, Lawrence H. Domash, and John T. Farrow (Los Angeles: MIU Press, 1974).

a grant of $21,540 to help train 120 secondary school teachers to teach SCI in high schools.

(The above information was compiled and disseminated by the MIU and is documented.)

There is much ongoing research in the educational field on the following subjects: TM and its effects on the mentally retarded child; efficacy of TM for language-learning ability; TM and the reduction of tension in college students; TM and the relationship of students with parents, teachers and peers; TM and creativity in students; TM and scholastic aptitude, etc. More and more colleges are accrediting the SCI courses within their curriculum. Things seem to look optimistic for SCI all the way, because the more research data that comes in the more the needle seems to point to better results among those who practice TM as opposed to nonmeditators.

Young people have certainly shown tremendous enthusiasm for TM and it is catching on in the older groups. The median age has changed in the last few years from twenty-three to thirty-three. The more generally accepted it is by the Establishment on local, state and national levels, the more available it will become.

The SCI movement has a world plan that hopes to encompass every country and have a teacher of SCI for every thousand people in the world. They have plans for a global television system and an international education system that encompasses all fields of study and endeavor. If the message they were propounding were anything except "Know thyself" and "Love thyself" it might cause some concern, but all you have to do is spend time around this dedicated selfless band of kindly, interesting and intelligent individuals, feel the inner peace and serenity they generate, and you realize your doubts are baseless. They are not trying to take over the world or force the world to accept *their* way of life or system of living; they are merely trying to strengthen the individual and help him to realize his full potential. I am such a notorious skeptic that I find it almost impossible to believe that it will happen, that their goals will be achieved (at least not in my lifetime), but I feel with all my heart that it is a step in the right direction if we are going to survive and avoid the holocaust, apocalyptically speaking. I close this section with a thought from *Buddhism and Zen:*

> The superior man, as soon as he hears of the path, earnestly practices the teaching: the average man, hearing of the path, sometimes remembers and sometimes forgets it: the inferior man, hearing of the path, ridicules it.

GETTING THERE

RESIDENCE COURSE

14

DURING the six times you have to attend the Introductory Classes to complete the TM course you can't help but see notices on the bulletin board about Residence Courses quoting price changes and other pertinent data about special lectures, meetings, guest appearances, etc.

On further inquiry I learned of two places in the immediate area where one could attend these courses: Litchfield, Connecticut and Livingston Manor, New York. The prices for attending these places range from forty-five dollars for a single room for the weekend (from Friday night to Sunday after lunch) session to several hundred dollars, depending on the length of stay and the seminars that are included. The several hundred is for a stay of many months that includes various degree courses in teaching TM and other activities, and pursuits in the Science of Creative Intelligence.

These weekend sessions are certainly not mandatory, but are made available for people who want to go deeper into the meditating scene—and for some, I suspect, who

197

just want to get away for a relaxing inexpensive weekend in the country complete with home cooked meals, lake, swimming pool and walks in the woods.

The weekend sessions are called "rounding" which means a structured two days of lectures, dining, exercises and meditating, all geared to send you back to the travail of your daily life sort of supercharged with tranquility. Most people that I spoke to, both at Livingston Manor and Litchfield, attended the weekend sessions approximately every three or four months. (After having spent the weekend I can say that I probably won't return—not because it was an unpleasant experience but simply for personality reasons. I happen to be one of those people who simply doesn't cotton too well to structured *anything*. I can't even enjoy being pampered on a timed daily regime at a fancy health farm; meals at certain times, baths at certain times, etc. don't appeal to me.)

Since the courses and prices are constantly changing I suggest, rather than my quoting any prices here and now which might be invalid by the time of printing, that anyone interested get in touch with the nearest TM centers for the latest details, which is what I did.

I called the Wentworth headquarters and they gave me the number for Livingston Manor because it is the weekend center nearest to my home. I then called Livingston Manor and made my reservation for what promised to be the first hot weekend of the season. I had already spent a day at the Litchfield Center, which happens to be just a stone's throw from my editor's country home, and I would like to say that it is a charming old Americana-type authentic country farmhouse complete with barns and outbuildings that have been lovingly transformed into quarters for dining, lectures, etc. What it hasn't got in the form of a swimming pool and lake it makes up for in good old country ambiance.

Spring had sprung with a vengeance on the Wednesday and Thursday before I went up to Livingston Manor, New York. The temperature had hit the eighties for two straight days and neither I nor the city were prepared. By Friday everyone, including myself, was ready to get to the country to see what nature had accomplished in the form of birds and blossoms. I was longing for the sweet smell of early lilacs and apple blossoms and a leisurely country walk by gurgling brooks leaping with legal trout. Right?

I woke up to a chilly Friday morning and a heavily overcast sky. By the time I hit the road a London fog had descended over the East River Drive, so heavy I almost overshot the George Washington Bridge approach. You could barely see the front of the car, let alone the blooming forsythia on the road banks. What was to be a glorious nature tour up the New York Thruway turned out to be a cold and miserable two-and-a-half-hour ride. I would have made it in shorter time but three-quarters of the way there the big Mercedes I had borrowed began to heat up at any speed over forty miles per hour. I pulled into the first gas station I saw. A grumpy-looking man approached and barked, "High test?" I smiled sweetly and told him I didn't need any gas, just water because the car was heating up.

He turned his back and walked back inside, saying gruffly, "We don't have water, just gas!" Luckily for him I had already done my twenty minutes TM or I'd have let him have my verbal mark of Zorro. As it was, I laughed and headed on up into the Catskills, meanwhile keeping on the lookout for another station.

I had spoken with the director of the Center in Livingston Manor on the phone earlier in the week to introduce myself, make my reservations and get directions to the Center, which is named Shankarachayra Nagar (meaning the first seat of learning. It used to be the old kosher hotel called The Waldemere). Just for the record, here are his directions: take the George Washington Bridge to Palisades Parkway north to New York Thruway as far as the Harriman exit. Turn right on 17 West to exit 96 and follow signs to the Academy for the Science of Creative Intelligence. (The signs just say "SIMS" or "Academy.")

In the Livingston Manor brochure it says that the Academy is located "on 460 acres of woods and meadows including a private 76-acre lake. The buildings rest on the side of a gentle hill above the lake and, from an elevation of 2,200 feet above sea level, provide an intensive view of the surrounding mountains of the Catskill Range. This beautiful setting is completely private and silent, yet is easily reached by car or bus."

I arrived early in the afternoon. There were others checking in at the same time, and there was some confusion about my reservation. This was cleared up with courtesy and expediency by a young lady at the desk. It being Friday afternoon, I inquired if there was a Mercedes dealer in the area to look at the car so that I could return to the city on Sunday without further trouble. The young lady said, "Oh, we have a mechanic right here to look at it, if you'd like?"

I said, "Fabulous, I'll wait for him outside by the car."

In a few minutes a nice young chap appeared, asked what the trouble was. He looked under the hood of the car, as I started up the motor for him. He fiddled around for a minute and said confidently, "It's your water pump. Can't get one around here but it will take you back to the city without any trouble, if you don't go too fast."

I thanked him and offered him five dollars for his trouble. He almost looked hurt. "No, I don't take money; it's my pleasure," he said, and disappeared toward the back of the hotel.

The lobby was spacious but unpretentious. There were posters and signs on a wall that served as a bulletin board

announcing coming events of interest in the TM movement. My room was in the executive wing located just at the
top of the stairs on the second floor. It was large enough to
accommodate a double chest of drawers, two armchairs,
two single beds *and* a double bed without being crowded.
It was clean and light, and furnished in the fashion of a good
middle class hotel. The bath was good sized and modern,
complete with clean towels, washcloths and individually
wrapped soaps and a fresh roll of toilet paper. I imagine at
the height of the season the old Waldemere charged at least
thirty-five dollars a night without meals for the accommoda-
tion. (And I was paying forty-five for the whole weekend
with meals.)

There were two mimeographed sheets of paper on top
of the chest of drawers welcoming me in the name of Jai
Guru Dev (Maharishi's guru in India and the man who, to
quote Maharishi, made him what he is) that listed helpful
suggestions and information to make my stay comfortable.
The first read as follows:

ACADEMY FOR THE SCIENCE OF CREATIVE INTELLIGENCE

Dear Meditators,

WELCOME TO THE ACADEMY FOR THE SCIENCE OF CREATIVE INTELLIGENCE, SHANKARACHARYA NAGAR.

To ensure that your stay with us will be a comfortable
and memorable one, we have listed a few suggestions
and information that we think might be helpful.

1. Due to the fact that the majority of meditators are
    nonsmokers, may we ask that you smoke in your
    bedroom only.

2. Please take care when burning incense and candles as we have a very limited crew of firemen.
3. Rearranging and moving furniture in your room is very strenuous; since you are here for rest, please enjoy our decorator's touch.
4. We want to keep our repairmen happily busy, so if you find any damages in your room please notify Housing.
5. Please don't use thumbtacks and nails in your room.
6. Moving to a new room? Check with Housing first.
7. Don't forget to check out with Housing and leave your key.
8. All SCI course participants may exchange linen and towels every Friday morning in the laundry, which is located in the basement.
9. All weekend course participants are asked to leave their used linen and towels outside their rooms before departing.
10. If you need any additional assistance, the Housing Office is ready to serve you. It is located behind the front reception desk and is open between the hours of 9:00 A.M. and 5:00 P.M., except on Thursday when the hours will be from 1:00 P.M. to 5:00 P.M.

JAI GURU DEV

The second read as follows:

ACADEMY FOR THE
SCIENCE OF CREATIVE INTELLIGENCE
Shankaracharya Nagar

Dear Meditator,

We are pleased to welcome you to Shankaracharya Nagar, our new Academy for the Science of Creative

Intelligence. We are certain that you will enjoy a relaxing and enlightening course. To help ensure the privacy of each individual and to accommodate each of you most comfortably, we ask that you observe these few suggestions.

It is important that the level of noise be minimal in the living quarters of the Academy. Since the walls between rooms are very thin, an effort should be made to be reasonably quiet in the rooms and hallways so that any disturbances can be avoided. Take special care to close your door quietly.

Please refrain from smoking anywhere other than your room.

If you have arrived by car, please park in our rear parking lot. The front drive must remain open for emergency equipment. Thank you for your cooperation.

ASSISTANCE
There is an "assistance form" at the front desk on which you may report anything unsatisfactory about your room (repairs, etc.) or request anything you may need (e.g. light bulbs, blankets).

ACADEMY BOOKSTORE
Our bookstore is located in the lobby across from the main desk. It is open from 1:30—2:30 on Saturday, Sunday, and Wednesday. Books, pamphlets and research literature dealing with TM are available as are supplies, toiletries and other items.

SCHEDULE
Meetings will be held in the second floor lecture hall, unless otherwise specified.

FIRST DAY (Friday)	DAILY SCHEDULE (Saturday)	LAST DAY (Sunday)
Dinner 6:30-8:00	Meditation . . .	Meditation . . .
Meeting 8:30-10:00	Breakfast 9:00-9:30 (cold only)	Breakfast same
Āsanas Demonstration 10:15	9:30-10:30 (hot & cold)	Meeting same
		Lunch same
	Meeting 11:00-1:00	Checkout after lunch
	Lunch 1:00-2:00	
	Meeting 2:30-4:00	
	Meditation . . .	
	Dinner 6:30-7:30	
	Meeting 8:00-10:00	

CHECKOUT

When you are ready to check out, place sheets and towels inside a pillowcase and leave them outside your door. After lunch, return your key to the front desk and your deposit will be refunded.

I felt a bit like I was back in Girl Scout camp after reading the do's and don'ts and the posted time for meals, meetings, etc.

I wanted to call the desk to see if I could talk to the director but quite understandably the phones had been removed from the rooms. How can you meditate if the phone's ringing? I unpacked my few belongings and went back downstairs in search of Ken Ross, the director to whom I'd spoken on the phone.

I followed a young lady through a maze of busy offices

full of modern equipment, IBM Selectric typewriters, mimeograph machines and even a Telex, which Ken explained to me was for quicker communication with their international headquarters in Switzerland and the other nerve centers of the movement in California, Chicago, etc. He was a very personable young man of twenty-four. He introduced me to his young wife who was working the Telex.

Having at one point in my varied career run a small resort hotel and restaurant, I was curious and questioned him about the management of such a large place (over 350 rooms). He informed me that although he had never had any hotel training (his training was a University of Wisconsin degree in psychology and European history), he ran the entire place with a volunteer staff of 40 whereas the management of the old Waldemere had a staff of over 180. They had taken over only six months ago and were in the process of doing some major improvements: redecorating, winterizing and renovating. The original buildings were about sixty years old. The main building was surrounded by smaller outbuildings that appeared to have sprouted from the ground in various stages of disrepair. I did a rough estimate in my head and figured it would take at least $300,000 to get the grounds and building into tip-top shape if you moved a crew of professionals in the next day. I mentioned this to him and he just laughed and said, "Well, there's no hurry. In time and with the help of the people here we'll get it all done. We have carpenters, plumbers, painters, grounds keepers, all in the TM movement. It will happen."

Just the cost of the paint alone would be staggering but when I mentioned that he didn't seem at all concerned. He and his wife explained in glowing terms the plans to make Livingston Manor the main branch of the Science of Creative Intelligence for the eastern part of the United States and their hope that eventually it would be accepted as an accredited university by the State of New York.

Before I could finish questioning them he excused himself, saying, "I'm sorry but we'll have to cut this short now because it is time to do our meditation."

That left me with about an hour before dinner, which I proceeded to use inspecting the rest of the main building. The corridors went on and on and on for about two city blocks. I peeked into several rooms that were or were not occupied by residence instructors and pupils. Many had poems or pictures on their doors. All were freshly painted and well kept. Some were full of people having tea and discussion groups. I passed busy, busy offices where they were preparing brochures, video tapes, lectures, music compositions; there were editorial departments and art departments. They were staffed by professionals in each branch: sound engineers, video engineers, cameramen, producers, composers, musicians, etc.—all in the TM movement. It truly looked like a functioning operation center that was out to accomplish big things. Everyone I spoke with was brimming with energy and enthusiasm for their particular projects.

At seven-thirty I went down to the main dining hall for dinner. It was a large room with windows overlooking the lake. It might have been able to seat over 500 people but the 80 or 90 people there were scattered at random. A long table in the center was set up cafeteria style. I picked up my cutlery and plate and hit the line. I heaped it with a marvelous fresh zucchini quiche, baked potato with sour cream, fresh Brussels sprouts with butter, a rice concoction, fresh garden salad with various bowls of nuts and bean sprouts to sprinkle on top, freshly baked blueberry cake topped with whipped cream. Coffee, tea or milk were offered. When my platter was overflowing I looked around for a table of interesting looking people to sit with. (No special seating assignments were indicated.)

I chose a table by the window at which were seated two or three older people; an attractive gray-haired Englishwoman, better dressed than most of the people there, smiled and welcomed me to the table. There was another woman of about thirty-five and a handsome, rugged-looking man of about forty-five. Apparently they were all strangers to one another. The small talk was about how long each of us had been doing TM, where we came from, etc. Apparently we were all there alone, without family or lovers.

The thirty-five-year-old woman was most loquacious. She said she had been in TM for over six months and had stopped going to her "head shrink" because she didn't feel the need for him any longer. She was a divorcée who ran her own successful travel agency. The rugged-looking man said he was an on-the-job construction engineer who lived in Greenwich, Connecticut. He said he had read about TM in the newspapers in conjunction with a business symposium. He had been in TM about two months and already he was beginning to notice changes in himself.

"Like what?" I asked.

"Well, for instance, I bought myself a motorbike, a Honda, and I go riding after work on it. I feel about twenty years younger. I've become interested in things that I had either lost interest in or never had any interest in before I started meditating, like the theater and reading. I really didn't know what kind of rut I was in and now I'm beginning to really feel alive again. It really is funny. My wife thinks I've got another woman. She doesn't believe the change in me."

I said, "Is she here with you?"

He looked kind of strange. "No, no, she isn't."

I hadn't meant to make him sad or anything, so I tried to lighten the situation. I laughed and said, "What makes you think she believes you really are here at a center for meditation instead of spending the weekend with another woman?"

Without hesitation he simply said, "She doesn't care," and turned back to the business of eating his food.

I turned to the good-looking, gray-haired woman.

"How long have you been meditating?" I asked her. She flashed me a beautiful smile and said quietly, "Fourteen years."

"Fourteen years," I repeated loudly. "Why that's longer than anyone I've ever spoken to." That really excited me. She would be the perfect person to interview. She must have all kinds of fantastic experiences and information for me. What a case study!

I blurted out, "Look, I'm doing a book on TM and I'd love to interview you this weekend. . . ."

The beautiful smile faded as rapidly as it had come. She shook her head. "No, no, I'd rather not," she said in a tone just weak enough to make me think with a little coercion I might convince her.

"Oh, please, I won't use your name if you don't want me to . . . ," I said as beguilingly as I could.

But she was adamant. She finished her dessert and left.

The remaining woman at the table was quite taken with the fact that I was a writer. She couldn't understand why the other woman wouldn't want to tell *me* all, since she had freely discussed her unique story *before* I sat down with them. However, by then it was lecture time and we all had to go.

After the lecture those of us who had never before attended a residence course assembled back in the dining hall to be shown how to do the *āsanas* and *prānāyāma* (yoga exercises and breathing techniques, which I'll explain later, that are a *voluntary* part of the "rounding"). As we entered we were all handed mimeographed instruction sheets explaining in words and diagrams the exercises that were about to be demonstrated. A "round" consists of approximately ten minutes of the *āsanas* or physical yoga exercises, followed by approximately four to five minutes of the simple breathing exercise *(prānāyāma)* followed by meditation (twenty minutes) followed again by *prānāyāma*. That constitutes one round.

One is advised to do *āsanas* before bathing or at least not to bathe immediately after the exercise; to dress loosely to allow freedom of movement; to do the āsanas at least forty-five minutes before the evening meal; to do the *āsanas* only once a day except during residence course when twice is allowed; to wait half an hour before doing *āsanas* after drinking liquid, at least one hour after a light meal, and at least four hours after a heavy meal.

The rugged gentleman with whom I had shared the dinner table and I gravitated toward one another. (I think it was more "safety-in-the-same-generation" attraction than romantic.) A lanky, agile young redheaded chap demonstrated the various postures of the *āsanas* with the natural dexterity of youth.

I mentioned to my companion that some of the postures would be damned difficult if not impossible for me owing to my "bad back." He nodded sympathetically and confided that he, too, suffered from a "bad back." The white glow of the full moon over the Catskills was beckoning me through the large windows. It had been a long day for both of us. He suggested we step outside and have a cigarette before bedtime. I readily agreed. Our few months of TM had not, as of that evening, done much for either of us in our attempts to give up smoking. We discussed the fact that we both felt like bad kids sneaking a smoke, knowing how bad it was for us. Then, off to bed. I was tired and slept like a baby in the clear, crisp air.

I awoke to a beautiful, cloudless sunny day. I thought about trying to do the āsanas, remembered my bad back, decided against it, did my meditation and headed down for breakfast.

There were about thirty people scattered about the huge dining hall. The food table offered a choice of yogurt, assorted nut meats, fresh fruit, hard and soft boiled eggs, scrambled eggs, a glorious assortment of about four or five different kinds of homemade bread and jellies, butter, honey, coffee, tea or milk.

I carried my plate to an empty window table. A lot of conversation in the morning, especially with strangers, has never been my forte. There were three or four young children across the room with their young parents making young-children noises. Ethnically speaking the diners were nondescript except there wasn't even a token black attending the course. (I checked up on this and found that there were indeed several black teachers of TM and that blacks as well as whites do attend residence courses.) As I was finishing my final cup of coffee I was joined by two very tall, very handsome young men who politely asked if it was OK if they sat with me. I was delighted.

In the course of our conversation I discovered they were both star basketball players and had both been offered professional contracts when they finished school this year. We had only a few minutes to talk before the morning lecture, but one boy expressed some concern with continuing meditating because he was afraid it was removing some of his aggressive tendencies and was afraid that would adversely affect his game. I walked away from them wondering the same thing and promised myself I'd try to find out more about that aspect of TM. (I later spoke with the head of the TM Physical Fitness Division, Don Leopold, about this. He said, "You're not the first person to ask that question. I can answer you that, on the contrary, by practicing TM your aggressions are channeled to the right place, *against your opponents and not against yourself or your friends.*")

I left the lecture early because I learned they were showing a video tape of a lecture I had already heard in an advanced session at the Wentworth. It was such a glorious day I decided to take a short drive down into Livingston Manor to check out the town.

I had naturally forgotten to pack my toothpaste and my first stop was the local pharmacy. Being a city slicker for so many years, I had almost forgotten what an old-fashioned country drugstore can be like. As I walked through the door the smell brought back an unmistakable *déja vu:* the antiseptic concoctions of the drugs comingling with the chocolate syrups of the soda fountain; the ancient light fixtures, the outdated, dusty wooden showcases; and the old down-east druggist dispensing his time-honored advice sought after by locals that wouldn't dream of bothering the M.D., who would undoubtedly send them a bill for it. While he was in the middle of totting up my order, the phone rang.

Bear in mind I was dressed in clean, simple Levi's, a leather jacket and moccasins. Nothing out of the ordinary for a country town.

His conversation went something like this . . . "Yes, Ted, I understand." Pause while Ted talked. "Yesss, well, all I can tell you is Joe went up there and it cured his acne and his bad back. The only trouble he had was with his wife and he couldn't get her to go. . . ."

Pause while Ted talked, then the old druggist leaned

his head out from the back room and spoke to me. "Do you know the phone number up there?" I looked around to see to whom he was talking. There was no one else in the place, so he was obviously talking to me.

"Up where?" I asked.

"Up to the Academy," he said, like I was a boob.

"No, no I don't," I said, shaking my head and wondering how he knew I was staying there. "But I'm sure it's in the book."

He shook his head and stuck his head back out of sight. "No, Ted, she don't have the number but I'm sure the operator can give it to you." Pause while Ted talked, then, "Yeah, well, all I can say is, it sure helped Joe." Pause. "Don't mention it, Ted. See ya around."

After I got over being a little put out by being spotted as "one of them," I couldn't help laughing because it reminded me of when I was a kid and how easy it was to spot a stranger in town or, during our county fair, the advance men for the carnivals. "Carney folk," we used to call them. It was also interesting to notice how the town people had accepted the academy and were actually recommending it —a giant step for small town folk, particularly mountain people.

At lunch the "other woman" joined me. She was interested to know if the Englishwoman had consented to be interviewed yet. I had to admit defeat. She said, "That's really a shame. Her story is fascinating. I'll see what I can do for you. . . ." I told her I'd appreciate it and the conversation turned to other things.

Saturday night and everyone was aflutter because the after-dinner lecture was to be by a psychiatrist from Yale who had written a book about the benefits of meditation, a live, honest-to-God lecturer as opposed to an instructor-videotape lecture. The instructors had publicized it well. I had been led to believe the attendance would be standing room only, so I finished dinner early and headed for the Oval Room, which used to be the old Waldemere discotheque, to get a good seat because I wanted to tape him.

As it turned out there was no need for that because the Oval Room was nowhere near filled when the lecture began. Apparently many of the meditators had heard the lecture before. Several minutes before the lecture began I noticed the Englishwoman enter the room, look around and head straight for the empty seat beside me. My hopes rose. Now, maybe, I could talk her into that interview. I was even more intrigued by what the other woman had said: "Fascinating story." What could it be?

She smiled as she sat down. I smiled back. "Lovely evening," I said. "Yes, isn't it?" she said. A long silence ensued. Finally I said, "Have you thought about that interview? I'd really appreciate it. . . ."

She thought for a moment and said, "Really, there's nothing much to tell. I started with Maharishi himself in London fourteen years ago, he was my instructor. . . ." Her eyes softened, a musing smile crossed her face. "What a lovely man he is . . . so extraordinary, so brilliant and so charming. . . ."

There was a stir in the room. Dr. Bloomfield, the lecturer, had arrived. I could have killed him. What miserable timing, just when I was getting her to talk. But those were the breaks. The lights went down and his slide lecture began.

He started the lecture by stressing that the mind and the body, the psychological and the physiological, are interconnected. He used slides of graphs from studies conducted by different researchers on meditation and its benefits to prove his points, among which were: increased spontaneity, more capacity for intimate contact, less anxiety, less bitterness, less guilt, less hostility, etc. He quoted from Freud and Jung, Fritz Perls of Gestalt therapy and Maslow, using various things they have said that led to his prime conclusion of the lecture: that all of them recognized a creative center in the human being, but in the seventy-five or so years of the practice and theory of psychoanalysis, no one had come up with a way of tapping this creative center. He finalized it by saying that more scientific evidence has surfaced in the three or four years of researching TM to show that meditation is a systematic way to reach our creative center and of reducing stress.

With all due modesty, I can assure you that I have explained these various points in greater depth and passion in this book than the learned doctor did in his lecture conducted with wooden pointer and picture slides, so I shall not tax you further with his verbatim quotes.

When he finished he asked if there were any questions. I was dying to ask him the question the young basketball player had mentioned about aggressiveness, but try as I might to get his attention, he concluded the session before he recognized my frantic hand waving in front of his face.

The Englishwoman and I walked back to the hotel together and I was hoping when we got there she would continue her story, but when we reached the lobby she dismissed me with a stifled yawn and said, "It must be the mountain air, I can hardly keep my eyes open . . . good night."

Sunday morning I noticed several of the middle-aged meditators walking a bit stiffly. The āsanas had taken their toll. When I spoke to my rugged friend he said kiddingly that he felt as though he had played four quarters as linebacker in a game with the New York Jets.

As I was finishing my breakfast I caught sight of the Englishwoman sitting alone at a corner table near the window. I gulped the last of my coffee and approached her. "Good morning," I said. "Do you mind if I join you for a cup of coffee?"

She was munching on a piece of toast but she shook her head and motioned for me to sit down.

Time was growing short. I knew this would probably be my last chance to be able to find out her experience with TM. I said, "Look, I have to leave before lunch. The other lady who sat with us Friday night said you had had a fascinating experience. Won't you tell me about it?"

She laughed. "Fascinating? I don't think it's that interesting to anyone but if you really want to know . . . it's just that my husband and I had been married for about three years. We both desperately wanted children but for three years we had not been able to conceive. We both went to doctors to see if there was any physical reason why we couldn't. Nothing, we were both perfect physical specimens.

"Well, about three years after our marriage I started meditating. As I told you, Maharishi was my teacher. Well, after six months of meditating I became pregnant and I now have three big strapping boys."

I said, "Yes, but couldn't the reason have been something else?"

She smiled and said, "Yes, we thought about that too. In fact, we were quite convinced that it was just one of those strange coincidences that happen. But then, my sister and her husband also had had difficulty conceiving children. I told her about what had happened to me. She thought about it for a while and then she started to meditate and within six months she too got pregnant."

I had to admit that sounded like more than just coincidence. I said, "Fourteen years is a long time. Didn't you ever feel like dropping out in all that time? I mean, didn't you ever get to the point where you thought it just wasn't helping?"

She thought that over for a minute before she answered. "Yes, yes I have. That's another strange thing. About three years after my first child was born I began to wonder if I was getting enough from it to take the time out of my busy day. By then I had a three-year-old and a one-year-old to take care of and finding the time was difficult. My husband and I were in Toronto on business. It was then I happened to notice in the paper that Maharishi was lecturing. I went to see him after the lecture. He remembered me. We had such a magnificent rapport and talking with him for those few minutes after the lecture gave me such strength and renewed faith in meditation that I've kept it up ever since. You must remember, in those days there were no centers or residence courses or instructors around for checkups. Once you learned it you were on your own until the next time you might just happen to be in the same town as Maharishi. And that time in Toronto really was a coincidence . . . or was it? I've often wondered."

ĀSANAS

15

IN Sri Aurobindo Ashram's glossary of Sanskrit terms, *āsanas* are defined as "Fixed posture: the habituating of the body to certain attitudes of immobility." By the practice of such postures, he contends, it "cures the body of restlessness, gives to it an extraordinary health, force and suppleness and seeks to liberate it from the habits by which it is subjected to ordinary physical Nature and kept within the narrow bounds of her normal operations." (Although there are over eighty different variations of postures in yoga, at the first residence course they only instruct you in the ten I will discuss, thank God—as you too will say if you are over twenty-five and you try to do them the first time.)

As I said, I never got around to doing the *āsanas* at the residence course because of my "bad back," but when I told this to my young editor, the slave driver, she was not exactly what you would call sympathetic. I wanted to just include the sheet of printed instructions and indistinct illustrations that had been given us at the residence course, but she was adamant. "Not on your life. Bad back or no bad back, I

217

want you to do those exercises and tell the reader how they go in your own words."

I pleaded, "But I'm forty-seven. I'm out of shape. . . ."

I was pleading to a deaf ear. I went to my agent for succor. I mean, isn't that what agents are for? Not this agent, not this time. She said, "If that's what they want that's what they want." I said, "Yeah, I'd like to see you try to do those bloody exercises . . ." (My agent is in worse shape than I am, outweighs me by about thirty-five pounds and is inches shorter than I am.) Succored I wasn't. She replied, "Exercise is one thing that isn't included in my measly ten percent. You're on your own, so you may as well get to it."

Right. Here we go:

Well, before we start, they caution you that it is better to do the postures of āsanas after bathing (but not immediately after) and before breakfast, to dress in loose garments to allow freedom of movement, and to move slowly in every case. *Sudden movements should be avoided at all times.* (This author's italics, lest you wind up as a permanent pretzel.) Also, they warn not to force or strain—VERY IMPORTANT (their caps); in time the body becomes more flexible, and you will soon be able to do the exercises naturally and properly with practice.

Are you ready? Hip, hip, let's go! Started 11:05.

I. *Tone up:*

(a) Get comfortably seated on the floor, preferably on a carpet if you are bony. Place both the palms and fingers of each hand on top of your head, and gradually press and release, moving hand pressure forward over the face (pressing and releasing all the time), eventually reaching over the face and then onto the neck and chest. (Women can take this opportunity for a daily breast lump check.)

(b) Press top of head with palms and fingers (both

hands) down over the back of head and neck and come around to the chest.

(Our instructor said that the purpose was to get the blood flowing always toward the heart, i.e., every move started above the heart works downward toward the heart and conversely, all movements started below the heart work up toward the heart.)

(c) Grasp fingertips of right hand with palm and fingers of left hand (left palm faced down) gradually moving the (press and release) pressure upward along arm to the shoulder and chest.

(While doing all this I more or less felt myself as a tube of toothpaste squeezing my thick blue blood ever heartward.)

(d) Repeat movement (c), reversing hands, etc.

(e) With tips of the middle fingers meeting horizontally at the navel, both hands resting on abdomen, press and release the abdomen, gradually moving hands (and pressure) up toward heart, reaching almost to chest.

(f) Using both hands, begin press-release procedure up the middle of the back and ribs toward the heart, as far as you can reach.

(g) Beginning with right foot, grasp top of toes with right hand and the sole of that same foot with the left hand. Press-release, gradually moving up to the calf, thigh and on to the waist.

(h) Repeat same with left foot.

(i) Lie on your back, draw both knees chestward and clasp hands over them. Raise head slightly.

(j) Starting from that position, roll to extreme right until right wrist touches the floor (here I experienced some extreme pain because I had neglected to take a massive nubby silver bracelet off and it began to cut into my wrist, so be sure to take off any and all jewelry that could hang you up or become knobby under you), then roll to extreme left by pushing up with right elbow and moving head to left. Repeat ten times in each direction.

Their instructions say that after that you are "to gradually asume a full prone position, relaxing completely but slowly." And believe me, after that you are ready to assume a full prone position and stay there for a spell until you get your breath back.

Okay? So much for getting the heart started or, as they call it, the "Tone-up."

II. *Second Position:* Kneel down. Sit your behind on the flat of your feet, heels apart, big toes crossed. (Another author's note: At this juncture author got a cramp in her left big toe and had to uncross same, but I don't think it's too important if your toes aren't crossed so don't worry if it happens to you.) Now, toes crossed if possible, place your hands in your lap with your right hand on top of your left, palms up. Hold head, neck and spine in straight line for fifteen seconds. Repeat one to three times.

III. *Third Position:* Lie on your back. Place hands alongside of body.

(a) The TM instructions say "slowly raise feet to half vertical position." (According to "bad back" experts on the Barbara Walter's show, this is definitely a no-no position to be in so I modified the position of the legs to a ninety-degree position, straight up in the air.) Then raise the trunk of the body to a vertical position also until the chin presses against the chest, simultaneously raising the forearms to help support the back. By now your entire body should be as straight up in the air as possible, the back of the neck lying flat against the floor.

(b) Now, slowly lower the legs down *toward your head.* (Your eyes should now be looking at your knees and this should take the weight off your elbows also if you are doing it properly.) Maintain this pose for half a minute.

Here the instructions became so unclear to me that I untangled myself and raced down to the Hampton Bookmart and bought a book on yoga by Yogiraj Sri Swami Satchidananda that much better illustrated the pose and how to attain it. Here Swami says, "Breathe normally while retaining the pose." He cautions: "Keep the mouth closed. If saliva collects, do not swallow but dispose of it after pose is finished." He also gets into other possible emergencies like sneezing, coughing or yawning and warns against doing them while "in pose." Come down immediately and then do what you have to do. He also warns against practicing this pose if there is a "disturbance in the organs of the head or if headache or fever is present." He contends this is a great exercise for regulating sex glands, blood circulation, seminal weakness (I had to look that up and Webster's says it relates to the semen), and feminine disorders. He goes on to say that it helps to cure the following: asthma, liver and intestinal disorders, dyspepsia, constipation, hernia, diabetes, heart troubles, urinary disorders, piles, varicose veins, and leprosy; and it helps reduce abdominal fat. He quotes the yoga name for the pose as *Sarvāngāsana,* which means "a beneficial pose for the whole body," and says it also tones up the thyroid gland.

(c) Now, slowly return to original position by bending the knees to balance the trunk of the body until the buttocks touch the floor, then straighten the legs and lower them slowly. Gradually relax. Start with a half minute and gradually increase to two minutes during one month.

IV. *Fourth Position:* Here's the one that kind of tickled me. The instructions say:

(a) Sit and stretch right leg (men, left leg). ??? (Author's question marks.)

(b) Bend the other leg so that the heel touches the perineum. (Just to make sure, the author looked up last word in above sentence and it meant what I thought it did: according to Webster it is "the area between the anus and the posterior part of the external genitalia esp. in the female.") Right, so in other words, your heel is in the center of your crotch.

(c) Bend forward and catch the center of the right foot with both hands, arms stretched.

(d) Draw in the lower abdomen and touch knee with forehead.

(e) Return to original position after five to fifteen seconds. Do same with other leg. Relax gradually, Repeat one to three times. (I had trouble with this so remember, do not force it; if you can't keep your leg straight when you do this, bend it to make it easier on yourself. This really pulls on the muscles at the back of thigh. I promise you, next year it will be easier.)

V. *Fifth Position:* This is somewhat similar to Number Three, except your legs go all the way back over your head until they touch the floor and your arms wind up crossed over your head. To start:

(a) Lie on back, arms at sides.

(b) Raise legs in straight position, then let them continue on up and behind your head until the toes touch the floor.

(c) Push the feet out as far as possible, making chin touch chest. Then cross arms over head. Hold for five seconds.

(d) Slowly return to original position by bending knees

to maintain balance of trunk until buttocks touch floor. Then straighten legs and lower them slowly. Relax. Repeat one to three times.

VI. *Sixth Position:* Satchidananda calls this "The Cobra Pose."

(a) Lie face downward, forehead touching the floor. Place palms on floor below corresponding shoulders so the back may be lifted to the middle part of the backbone. Keep legs close together, toes pointed.

(b) Slowly raise head and chest bending neck back as far as possible. Then slowly raise chest, vertebrae by vertebrae. Lower part of body, from navel to toes, should be touching floor. Maintain posture for fifteen to thirty seconds.

(c) Return to original position, resting right or left cheek on floor. Relax completely. Repeat one to three times.

VII. *Seventh Position:* This one really is rough if you have a bad back.

(a) Lie on chest.

(b) Hold arms at your sides, palms up.

(c) Rest chin on floor.

(d) Raise the legs in a straight position as much as possible.

(e) Retain for a few seconds and return to original position. Repeat one to three times. They say that if you find it difficult raising both legs at once in the beginning, raise one, bring it down, and alternate with the other four to six times.

VIII. *Eighth Position:* This is literally the *pièce de résistance* or, as Swami calls it, "The Half Spinal Twist." Good luck.

(a) Sit with right leg stretched forward on floor.

(b) Raise left leg so that foot is on floor near right knee (about a foot and a half in front of buttocks).

(c) Turn your trunk to the left, pressing the right forearm against the outside of the left thigh, close to the knee, with the sole resting gently on the floor. Right knee should be close to chest. Now, with the same right hand, grasp the right leg below the knee.

(d) Put the left hand around your back onto the right thigh. (Now, do you see what I meant by a permanent pretzel?)

(e) Turn trunk and head to left.

(f) Maintain pose for a few seconds and come back slowly to original position. If you can get untangled, repeat with other leg.

IX. *Ninth Position:* This one's easy.

(a) Standing position, feet together, legs stretched.

(b) Bend forward till your hands touch your toes (or as close as you can get), arms stretched and forehead nearly touching the knees or nearly above them, drawing in the abdomen. Hold for five seconds, repeat one to three times.

X. *Tenth Position:* This one you're going to love because it was my favorite.

(a) Lie down flat on the floor on your back and relax, leaving the mind and body loose for a few minutes.

(b) That's all there is to it!

Now for the *prāṇāyāma* or breathing exercises. These are fun and easy, and to be done after the *āsanas* and prior to meditation.

Prana is a Sanskrit word meaning our life force or life energy or life stuff, if you will. Swami Satchidananda says we can live without food and water for days, for minutes without air, but not for a second without *prana*. He contends that by the regular practice of *prāṇāyāma* we can store the life force in our system and even mentally transmit it to others, like the touch healers. Breathing is the external manifestation of *prana*. We breathe in about fifteen times a minute, and in one inhalation and exhalation is about a pint of air. By deep breathing he says you can supercharge the blood with oxygen and thereby bring extra life to the body.

(a) Sit in a comfortable position.

(b) Take the right thumb to the right nostril and close it.

(c) Breathe out through left nostril slowly and completely.

(d) Noiselessly breathe in through same nostril. When you crest, close left nostril with the ring and middle fingers of the right hand while opening the right nostril to exhale.

(e) Breathe out noiselessly, slowly, and completely from the right nostril.

(f) Breathe in again through right nostril the same way.

(g) Repeat process for four to five minutes.

Now you do your meditation for twenty minutes. After that is done you have completed what they call a "round."

At the residence course you do a round in the morning and a round in the evening; and believe me, after that and dinner, you are ready for beddy-bye and the best night's sleep you have had in a long time.

As I said before, neither these residence courses, the advanced lectures or the *āsanas* and *prāṇāyāma* are necessary to practice TM and benefit from it. They do, however, serve as refreshers of enthusiasm and tend to give one a little bolstering up if you find your meditating spirit is beginning to lag, which sometimes happens after one has been meditating for a while. In the beginning the change is dy-

Chart 34

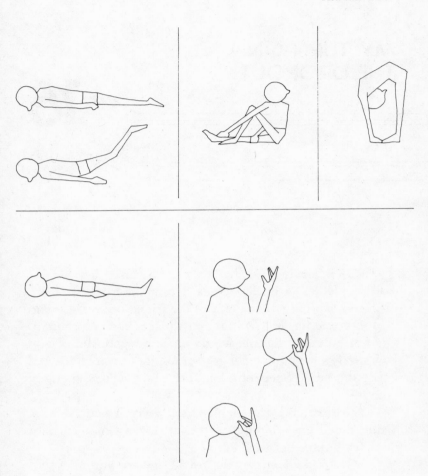

namic enough to keep you aware of the difference, but as time goes on you become used to the benefits, and as their dynamism seems to lessen, one's enthusiasm may be inclined to wane, like getting used to a love affair. Therefore, to place yourself, immerse yourself again among the active devotees can only help to restimulate your interest and confirm the goals you were searching for in the first place.

MY TURN-ON,
THE DROPOUT

16

B EFORE leaving for Livingston Manor I had what I
thought was a brilliant idea. I remembered that Faith
Winston, who, if you recall, was the friend of Helen's who
had interested us in TM in the first place, lived en route to
the Catskills and that she would make a wonderful person
to interview for my book. I got her number from Helen and
made the call to Sneeden's Landing which went something
like this:

She answered, I recognized her voice. I said, "Hello,
Faith, this is Pat Hemingway. I met you in Connecticut at
Helen's house that weekend. . . ."

"Of course I remember you. How are you?"

I could tell by her tone she couldn't imagine why I was
calling her after all this time.

I said, "I don't know whether or not Helen told
you, but I am writing a book about TM and thought
since you were sort of responsible for my getting involved, you would make a marvelous interviewee. In
fact, I'm on my way to a residence course upstate and

228

thought, if you're not busy on Sunday, I could stop by on my way home. . . ."

I heard a kind of strange groan on the other end of the wire. I hastened to add, "Look, if it's not convenient, don't hesitate to say so and we can make it for another time . . . I realize it's rather short notice."

There was a hesitation before she said, "Oh, dear, oh, er, ah, *gee Pat,* I'm afraid I have bad news for you . . ."

My instant reaction was that something had happened to either her husband or her kids but she continued, "You see, I've ah, I've dropped out. I mean, I don't meditate any longer." She said it as though she had let *me* down.

I was stunned for a moment but since I was paying for the call I recovered somewhat quicker than I might have, "Whaaaat?" I screamed. "You can't do thaaat . . . ," my voice trailing off into a whimper. For an instant I was terribly disappointed but then I thought: How terrific! How ironic! The person who was resonsible for my starting has dropped out! The book needs a dropout and what better person to tell me *why* one would drop out? I mean, there are no meeting places where *ex*-meditators congregate that I had ever heard of . . . where would I even look for one? And Faith was just right—perfect, matter of fact. She's about forty years old, upper-middle class, Smith graduate, happily married, four children, healthy and beautiful, plenty of money, talented successful artist, well-read, articulate, aware and concerned about her life, her family and the world in general . . . just perfect.

Perhaps too exuberantly, I said, "That's fabulous, just fabulous. . . ."

I detected a flicker of doubt on the other end and hastened to say, "I mean I'm sorry you dropped out, but at least if you let me interview you I can find out *why* and that's important for the book, don't you think?"

She laughed good-naturedly. "God, you writers. There's nothing sacred. . . ."

We set up the meeting for Sunday afternoon at her home.

In contrast to the cold, rainy ride up to the Catskills, Sunday morning was sunny and bright. The foliage had greatly benefited from the weekend downpour and was brilliantly coloring the countryside. The Winstons lived in Sneedens Landing, just off the Palisades Parkway on my way home to New York.

Faith had given me explicit directions. One hour and a half after leaving Shankar I was driving up a bough-covered lane that I hoped led up to the Winstons' compound. I say compound because as you entered the clearing, to the left was a small white frame house that was obviously too small to be the main house, probably the handyman's cottage. Off to the right was a large yellow brick kiln and there were Faith's great cast-cement sculptured spheres, artistically arranged in groupings about the green lawn. Snuggled back among the tall pines and lush poplars I spied the house.

Actually it was a many-gabled, stately, rambling barn that had been handsomely transformed into their residence, each gable incorporating large random-shaped panes of glass which lent a modern air to the old building.

Toting my trusty tape recorder I followed the winding flagstone path to what appeared to be the front door. As I approached, the door opened and Faith warmly welcomed me into her big old country kitchen, complete with fat calico cat nestled down into a comfy overstuffed chair. The second I walked through the door I was aware of the sense of love and warmth that makes a house a home. There were growing things wherever one's eyes happened to fall, green flowering plants on the floor, on the windowsills, hanging from the lovely old beams; on the floor near the door was an open cage full of platinum blonde-baby chicks peeping away for dear life; overhead hung a cage of multicolored cockateels. Wherever I looked there was the flow of life, of healthy living things, thriving—a glowing tribute to its mistress. I said as much. Faith smiled shyly, waved her hand and muttered, "Oh, the children take care of most of them. . . ."

We settled down at the big kitchen table. She made us a cup of coffee, while I got my tape recorder set up.

I said, "All right, down to business. Let's see, the last time we saw each other you had been meditating for about three months, and you were so turned on by it you managed to turn Helen and me on. What happened? Why did you stop, and when did it happen?"

She sat for a moment collecting her thoughts. I could see that "dropping out" had obviously disturbed her. She wasn't the type that started something and didn't finish it. It was against her nature. Everything I knew about her life attested to that.

She began slowly, low-keyed, "Let me start this way: at the point when I became interested in and started TM, my life was rather anxious and tense. From what I had heard about meditating I was terribly excited about it. In the beginning I felt quite changed and different. It is an amazing process. It did make me aware of a part of myself . . . a sort of central place that I was never aware of before. I still can be conscious of *that* if I stop to think about it and that's marvelous."

I asked, "Well, how did you stop? Did you stop abruptly?"

"Oh, I never intended to stop. I just found that I stopped. I didn't even notice *when* I had stopped! I remember I kept finding myself saying, 'Excuse me,' and having to leave whatever or whomever for twenty minutes. During that time I was eagerly doing it I didn't care because I cared about *it,* but I guess the caring faded—that began to loom larger than the benefits, the twenty minutes I absented myself from my guests or my chores.

"That twenty minutes was separate. I never felt it integrated into my life. Then, gradually, the novelty wore off . . . I gradually floated to the surface and eased off and that was the end of it."

She continued very thoughtfully, "I like the feeling that one's life is as integrated as possible and meditating began to seem like some funny, separate thing that I was doing. It didn't quite blend. I was hoping my life would somehow go in the TM direction. . . ."

I wasn't sure what she meant by "TM direction," so I asked her to clarify that statement.

"Well, I had hoped my life would blend the other direction . . . I like the idea of the serene, the more Eastern approach to life. What I am trying to say is my life is *Western,* the push and pull is *Western;* I had a sort of dream that TM would be a way of life. . . ."

I interrupted again. "Well, so do I, but I think we have to do it longer, much longer to achieve that kind of serenity. . . ."

She nodded. "Yes, I suppose I did what was typical (meaning drop out) because the experience didn't seem to me to be appreciably deepening. When I think about it I ask myself if I really did think that it was going to change me. Also, I didn't know anyone else who was doing it, none of my friends or acquaintances. I had a feeling of isolation. . . ."

I said, "That is why they say that a checkup is necessary once a month for the first year—to eliminate that feeling that you are alone. It is a kind of reassurance."

Faith mused, "Yes, now that you mention it I do remember the teacher talking about stopping—about how you forget how you felt before. But actually, I don't notice myself screaming at the children or feeling exhausted or fragmented."

I said, "I get such a jolt of energy."

"Yes, that's true, I remember feeling that. But my life happens to be on an up phase right now."

I didn't know her too well so I hesitated before I said, "Don't answer this if you think it's too personal, but I know you went to an analyst. Are you still going?"

"No," she replied, "that's a fair question, but the answer is no, I'm not still going."

I pursued, "Were you practicing TM when you went to her? Did you discuss it at all with her?"

Her face lit up. "Yes, that was interesting. She's a Freudian analyst, you know. And though she was aware of the use of TM in hospitals so it wasn't a new term to her, she kept misspeaking herself and calling it 'reflection' instead of meditation. She thought of it as a form of self-hypnosis. I know that the TM people have had that analogy posed to them before, so when I explained to her that in self-hypnosis one doesn't experience the same bodily changes—when you come out of self-hypnosis the same circumstances exist, nothing about you has changed nor has your approach to the existing circumstances—she didn't seem to, or want to, understand. She kept thinking it was a separate thing. She even likened it to merely postponing your life for those twenty-minute sessions, postponing your problems for those two periods of the day. Maybe without knowing it, without admitting to myself, I did think that she was right, that it was a separate thing and that it wasn't weaving into the rest of my life. . . .

"Anyhow, at the time I felt I explained to her the error of her thinking *once,* and I thought if she didn't or wouldn't understand the first time, at those prices I couldn't afford to try to explain the difference again. Actually I found her viewpoint quite negative."

At that moment her handsome husband walked in and fixed himself a drink. When he left the room I said, "It's too bad he didn't get interested . . . it might have helped."

She agreed. "Yes, well, he was marvelous. He never made fun of me or did anything that was at all discouraging. In fact, just about the time I stopped he was beginning to show some interest. God knows, he works so hard and his job is so trying he could certainly use something to relieve his stresses . . . but just then I stopped, so he kind of forgot about it."

I wish I could better express how benign, in the true sense of the word, her countenance was, as she sat across from me. So much so that I phrased my next question as carefully as I could.

I said, "Looking at your home, your world, your divine husband . . . your life here seems *el perfecto.* Have you *never* felt self-destructive?"

It was as though I had tilted the pinball machine. Everything on her face lit up. "No, no, that's not true. That's what I keep trying to tell you. I have a strong self-destructive streak. Okay, things are on the up now; things are going well but when they're not, I do have a self-destructive streak."

I interjected quickly, "Well, it doesn't show."

"Well," she said, "maybe I've been healed enough by professional help so it doesn't show, but if you had seen me twenty years ago. I was hell bent to destroy myself. I have been to shrinks now for many years, not all solid, five years here, three with that one, two another time . . ."

Again she stopped for a second to formulate her thoughts before she continued, "You see, as I realized that I was stopping TM I didn't feel I was quitting for good. When the subject comes up at friendly gatherings I always speak very highly of it; I never pooh-poohed it. I think I stopped because my life changed, evened out. I stopped going to my analyst about the same time I stopped meditating just like I started back at my analyst when I started TM.

"Actually, when I think about it, I feel that either one extreme or the other would lead me back [to TM]: one being crisis-time or a lot of tensions; or the other is, I keep seeing myself as somehow leading a peaceful, older existence where TM would fit in more naturally with a serene way of life—contemplative—so to speak. That sounds contradictory because I know in the hectic Western world TM is beneficial."

I hastened to assure her I knew exactly what she meant. I was in complete accord.

She laughed and said, "In the final analysis, I guess I'm a bit like those people who never set foot in a church until they feel they're in deep trouble. Then they run to church. And then, the minute they're out of trouble or the trouble passes, they forget about 'Ol' Christ' till the next time. Undoubtedly, I feel I'll probably begin to meditate again when the next emotional crunch strikes . . . and probably go back to my shrink as well."

About that moment the tape ran out and her husband ran in. "How would you girls like a drink?" Then he noticed the tape recorder. "Am I being taped?" I nodded. He laughed and said, "Gee, I'd better watch my expletives . . . or I'll get in trouble like tricky Dick."

Almost three months have now passed since that interview. I have given it a great deal of thought and since then have covered a lot of research ground on meditation, meditators and a few drop-outs.

First, I think two of the main factors of dropping out are *Time* and *Guilt*. I have joked about how difficult it is in this, our twentieth century world, to really find time for twenty minutes twice a day to devote to a totally "selfish" endeavor that is also so completely abstract in form. Although we don't seem to have to make excuses to watch TV endless hours on end, or for that matter, any other non-productive use of our time, some people definitely have a sense of guilt about taking the time out for TM. No one *wants* to feel guilty, so I can only conclude that when we miss doing our TM it does somehow make us feel guilty, that we have shirked our duty or some such nonsense. We don't approach it with the common sense that we would have missed going to church on a Sunday, simply because it is new and different and we are still ignorant of the results and goals early on in the TM game, so to speak. Therefore, many people gradually (or abruptly) stop meditating so they needn't feel guilty when they miss. And at the same time, they no longer have to feel guilty for absenting themselves from friends and family.

Next is *Necessity*. Many people take up TM because their lives are in a state of needing *something*, some more urgently than others. As Faith, our token dropout, said, people tend to forget about 'Ol' Christ except when they need him. I think many people who drop out of TM do so for the same reasons. The urgent need that drove them to try TM decreases (ironically enough because meditating lessens anxieties by its very nature), and then they stop meditating. Kind of like the tooth that stops hurting when you get to the dentist.

And finally, I believe many people, like Faith and even myself to some degree, are fascinated with the sense of the

Eastern forms of religion and philosophies. We have read some, enough to convince us that there is proof of the ability of the mind to reach higher levels of consciousness and greater levels of peace and tranquility of spirit. We would like to take a Jet plane to get there, if possible. But it is not possible.

It takes *time* to reach Transcendental Consciousness, more time to reach Cosmic Consciousness, even more for God Consciousness and many, many moons (maybe many lifetimes) to reach Nirvana.

As in any trip, it takes *time;* the farther you go the longer it takes. Also, the speed and effort with which you travel determines how fast you reach your destination. It is up to the individual what his destination or goal is and how much he wants to give up, to sacrifice, if you will, of the Western to reach the Eastern shores of wisdom.

It isn't necessary, or even probable, that one change his Western way of life in order to reach an understanding of those higher levels of consciousness. As I've said before, TM can be the bridge that combines the two worlds.

It is a long, time-consuming, mind- and effort-consuming process or series of processes to reach those higher levels of consciousness; and Western or Jet oriented as we are, we are unconditioned and unable to wait for long-term results. In our button-pushing conditioning we get impatient if we don't see instant results, like instant tea. But, as Faith said, people may return to TM later in life, when the pace of raising a family and pursuing a successful career has slowed or even stopped. Or, to put it another way, if you believe that there is a time for all seasons, then you will have reached the season for meditating.

COUNTDOWN
FOR BLISS-OFF

17

"GETTING THERE" implies that there are other ways to raise the consciousness level or level of awareness, or create an altered state of consciousness. There are very simple ways to alter your state of consciousness: the hallucinogens, the downies, the uppies, marijuana, the opiates; you can also get out there on too much or too little oxygen, by cutting off the blood supply to the brain for a short period of time, knocking yourself silly with a baseball bat, etc.

However, these are only temporary ways, and once the experience is over, it is over. What we are talking about is getting there and staying there so that your life is ever being sustained, enlightened and rewarded by your altered state of awareness of your life and the life that surrounds you. In other words, there are positive techniques, life-supporting techniques. Transcendental meditation is only one of many of these techniques. Some others you might be interested in looking into are:

(1) Fervent prayer or the constant repetition of prayer.

Some people do this so zealously that they enter into a self-hypnotic state.

(2) Isolation in remote, exotic places such as the sea or the desert or the mountains with no human contact. This a way to commune with nature, so to speak, to feel oneself in tune with the natural rhythm of the "world spirit" without the superimposed sounds and irritations of civilization intruding upon your solitude. John the Baptist went to the desert whenever he felt the need of cleansing his mind and spirit of worldly thoughts. Oftentimes, when I have been on a long auto trip traveling alone, I have found that after several hours of steady driving I can't for the life of me remember what, if anything, I had been thinking of those many hours: I have been in some sort of state of mental isolation, even though I was obviously automatically dealing with the other traffic in my habitual cavalier fashion.

I am also reminded of an open meeting of The Quiet Birdmen, a licensed pilot's organization, to which I was invited as the guest of a pilot friend of mine. Outside of the memory of meeting several of the best-looking men I had ever seen in one gathering, the one important, poignant memory of that occasion was the impellingly extraordinary look about their eyes, "Flyer's Eyes," as I thereafter called them. It was as though the focus of their eyes had some extra, unlimited vision that we less fortunate groundhogs were deprived of. Some people refer to it as "a faraway look in the eyes." Seafaring men have it, desert nomads have it, plains people have it, high mountain folk have it. People who live in constricted areas don't have it—their eyes are not accustomed to unlimited horizons. I bring this up here because in my recent experience and association with long-time practitioners of meditation I keep observing a similar look in their eyes, regardless of where their topographical home might be situated. For what my unsubstantiated observation is worth, I have yet to come across a "beady-eyed" long-time meditator. Unscientifically, I have concluded that meditation, over a period of years, brings to the meditator some kind of extended vision. Perhaps that is what is referred to in Eastern terms as "the third eye" or "the inner eye"!

(3) Self-hypnosis. You can be trained in this technique by a qualified hypnotist. I tried this in an effort to stop smoking. It cost me $75 in 1970, New York City prices. I neither learned to hypnotize myself nor did I stop smoking.

(4) Breathing. By changing the supply of oxygen to the brain you can alter your consciousness; if you send too much to the brain you can make yourself completely unconscious, or by sending too little you can achieve the same effect. Gaylor Hauser once told me that if I was emotionally upset over some specific thing, just take ten very deep breaths slowly and it would help. It does. It has an instant calming effect; even if you are on the verge of tears, it really works.

(5) Koan. A koan (Japanese) is a puzzle that doesn't seem to make any sense. It is used in certain forms of Zen. If you concentrate on the puzzle long enough, to the exclusion of all other thought, it has the effect on the mind and body of meditation and can alter your state of consciousness. It is used by the Sufis, the Hasidim, the Ch'an and Zen. For example: "What is the sound of one hand clapping?"

(6) Chanting, the endless repeating of a certain sound, sounds, tone or tones. The Hare Krishna singers are a good example of this method. In case you are not privileged to have a band of these chanters to observe in your town, in New York City on practically any street corner you might run into them. At first I thought that they numbered many because no matter what part of town I managed to be in they too were in evidence. But on closer observation I

realized that they were just as ubiquitous as myself, that they were the same bunch of saffron-robed young men and women with prison-pale faces and shaven heads, except for one long piece of pony tail that seems to be gathered together at the cowlick and flows down their necks. They have that faraway expression in their eyes too, which apparently stems from all that chanting and dancing up and down to the tune of "Hare Krishna, Hare Krishna, Hare Krishna," ad infinitum, from street corner to street corner, from morning to night. They cohabit but practice strict dietary and other social regimens that obviously include denouncing private material wealth. If you are interested in this, you can buy a record put out by Happening Records called *Krishna Consciousness,* and learn the chant so you can do it on any street corner in your home town. The robes are simple affairs that can be simulated by dying a sheet saffron yellow and draping yourself simply in it. As for shaving your head, don't forget to leave enough at the crown to make a good pony tail.

(7) Religous conversion. This has been going on for as long as recorded history. Attend enough present-day evangelical or holy roller meetings and desire enough, and you will probably experience this "ecstasy" that undoubtedly alters not only your consciousness but your entire mode of life. Charles Colson and Senator Hughes of Iowa are prominent examples of this.

(8) Dervish. We have all heard of the whirling dervishes. This is an ancient device that consists of spinning and turning the body endlessly around and around. It is still practiced in some parts of the world by a sect called the Sufis. In fact, in Turkey you can watch a dervish festival that lasts for two whole weeks. Try it for two whole hours and you'll see how it can alter your state of consciousness.

These are but a few ways to change your mind around.

In Edward Rosenfeld's *The Book of Highs,* he lists over 250 ways of altering your head without taking drugs. Seriously, though, most of the lasting religions through the ages have had some form of meditation as a part of their ritual. There are various methods of meditating besides using the mantra technique. Many can be self-taught. Had I wanted, I could have gone to the public library, spent a few hours boning up and probably taught myself to meditate, not only saving the price of the course but the cabfare and the time and effort to attend those six meetings, but I know myself well enough to know that, regardless of how much of an individual I think I am, I really belong to the vast majority of *Homo sapiens* who usually require outside discipline, structure and guidance to assist me in learning any intricate or complicated new subject. There is also the psychology working of having to put out the costly time, effort and hard cash that fulfills my old puritan ethic of something-for-nothing-is-worth-nothing and, conversely, since I did have to put forth those aforementioned valuables I am more prone to continue doing it. One other way that I believe makes me belong to the vast majority is that I usually approach any new course of action with some apprehension, if not downright fear of failing in what I set out to do. And like most people, I find that it is more supportive to begin these ventures in a group rather than by myself. That probably has something to do with the old "misery loves company" syndrome but whatever the reason it is nonetheless valid.

Last but not least of the reasons I opted for taking the TM course as opposed to either learning meditation by myself or by some other school was: (1) the offer of free followup checkups and refresher lectures; (2) there was no mandatory exercise, rigorous diet or other disciplinary regimen necessary to get the complete benefit from meditating (great amounts of self-discipline have never been my forte);

and (3) the money. The TM course is quicker, easier and less expensive than any of the other formal meditation instruction that I have heard about.

My fellow Sagittarian, Frank Sinatra, is credited with the expression, "I'm for anything that helps you through the night." Well, in my experience and observations, that's what TM does, helps you get through the days and nights a little better than you did before.

In my research for this manuscript I ran across a paragraph in a very esoteric book about Zen which I shall take the liberty to paraphrase:

> Unless you have faith in being enlightened in *this* life you had better not take up meditation at all. There are plenty of paths (sects, religions) you can follow which promise enlightenment *after* death . . . go to them and be happy. . . .

In conclusion, may I say to you what an old master once said to his disciples: "If you follow my instruction and do not achieve enlightenment, you may lop off my head!"

EPILOGUE

ODE TO ME
My One and Only, My Most Beloved Me

My one and only, my best beloved ME,
You, who forever keep my eyes half closed
That they may see only as *you* see
Who make my ears to hear only as *you* hear.
Oh, you, my savior from the Eternal,
My preserver from the Infinite,
You, who reveal life through the throb of fear,
You, *my one and only, my best beloved* ME,
To you, your abject voluntary slave,
I humbly bow . . .

From the huge threat of freedom you protect me,
My one and only, my best beloved ME,
Like some fierce lover, avid and commanding,
You possess me . . .
Instead of changeless infinite bliss you give me

244

The languor or violence of time-bound pleasure,
My one and only, my most generous ME.
You conquer when I love you
And when I hate you, you triumph still—
Your servant is my precious skin that wraps
The marvel of my body even for a hundred years—
Without you I would know eternity,
My one and only, my best beloved ME.
I would be all—fragrance and music, sea and sky . . .
ME, personal
ME, the unmatchable
ME, the captive
ME, ME, ME !

You make me capable of knowing—
But not of being.
Of possessing—
But not of being.
Of existing—
BUT NOT OF BEING !

Laura Archera Huxley
This Timeless Moment

APPENDIX:
REFERENCES FOR CHARTS

1. Bubble Diagram
   Reference: SIMS,
2. Decreased Anxiety
   Reference: Lawrence Farwell, "Effect of Transcendental Meditation on Level of Anxiety," *Scientific Research on Transcendental Meditation: Collected Papers Vol. 1,* eds. David W. Orme-Johnson, Lawrence H. Domash, and John T. Farrow. Los Angeles: MIU Press, 1974.
3. Increased Psychological Health
   Reference: Philip C. Ferguson and John C. Gowan, "The Influence of Transcendental Meditation on Anxiety, Depression, Aggression, Neuroticism, and Self-Actualization." Paper presented at California State Psychological Association, Fresno, California, 1974.
4. Rehabilitation of Prisoners III
   Second Reference: Monte Cunningham and Walter Koch, "A Pilot Project at the Federal Correctional Institute at Lompoc, California," *Scientific Research on Transcendental Meditation: Collected Papers Vol. 1,* eds. David W. Orme-Johnson, Lawrence H. Domash, and John T. Farrow. Los Angeles: MIU Press, 1974.

5. Change in Cardiac Output
   Reference: Robert Keith Wallace, "The Physiological Effects of Transcendental Meditation: A Proposed Fourth Major State of Consciousness." Ph.D. thesis, Department of Physiology, University of California, Los Angeles, 1970.

6. Faster Recovery from Sleep Deprivation
   Reference: Donald E. Miskiman, "The Effect of Transcendental Meditation on Compensatory Paradoxical Sleep," *Scientific Research on Transcendental Meditation: Collected Papers Vol. 1,* eds. David W. Orme-Johnson, Lawrence H. Domash, and John T. Farrow. Los Angeles: MIU Press, 1974.

7. Relief From Insomnia
   Reference: Donald E. Miskiman, "The Treatment of Insomnia by Transcendental Meditation," *Scientific Research on Transcendental Meditation: Collected Papers Vol. 1,* eds. David W. Orme-Johnson, Lawrence H. Domash, and John T. Farrow. Los Angeles: MIU Press, 1974.

8. Increased Orderliness of Thinking I
   Reference: Donald E. Miskiman, "The Effect of Transcendental Meditation on the Organization of Thinking and Recall (Secondary Organization)," *Scientific Research on Transcendental Meditation: Collected Papers Vol. 1,* eds. David W. Orme-Johnson, Lawrence H. Domash, and John T. Farrow. Los Angeles: MIU Press, 1974.

9. Increased Orderliness of Thinking II
   Reference: Donald E. Miskiman, "The Effect of Transcendental Meditation on the Organization of Thinking and Recall (Secondary Organization)," *Scientific Research on Transcendental Meditation: Collected Papers Vol. 1,* eds. David W. Orme-Johnson, Lawrence H. Domash, and John T. Farrow. Los Angeles: MIU Press, 1974.

10. Increased Orderliness of Thinking III
    Reference: Donald E. Miskiman, "The Effect of Transcendental Meditation on the Organization of Thinking and Recall (Secondary Organization)," *Scientific Research on Transcendental Meditation: Collected Papers Vol. 1,* eds. David W.

Orme-Johnson, Lawrence H. Domash, and John T. Farrow. Los Angeles: MIU Press, 1974.

11. Dualism
Reference: Robert E. Ornstein, *The Psychology of Consciousness,* W.H. Freeman & Co., The Viking Press, 1972.

12. Increased Strength and Orderliness of Brain Functioning I
Reference: Mark Westcott, "Hemispheric Symmetry of the EEG during Transcendental Meditation," *Scientific Research on Transcendental Meditation: Collected Papers Vol. 1,* eds. David W. Orme-Johnson, Lawrence H. Domash, and John T. Farrow. Los Angeles: MIU Press, 1974.

13. Increased Strength and Orderliness of Brain Functioning II
Reference: Mark Westcott, "Hemispheric Symmetry of the EEG during Transcendental Meditation," *Scientific Research on Transcendental Meditation: Collected Papers Vol. 1,* eds. David W. Orme-Johnson, Lawrence H. Domash, and John T. Farrow. Los Angeles: MIU Press, 1974.

14. Increased Strength and Orderliness of Brain Functioning III
Reference: Mark Westcott, "Hemispheric Symmetry of the EEG during Transcendental Meditation," *Scientific Research on Transcendental Meditation: Collected Papers Vol. 1,* eds. David W. Orme-Johnson, Lawrence H. Domash, and John T. Farrow. Los Angeles: MIU Press, 1974.

15. Increased Strength and Orderliness of Brain Functioning IV
Reference: Mark Westcott, "Hemispheric Symmetry of the EEG during Transcendental Meditation," *Scientific Research on Transcendental Meditation: Collected Papers Vol. 1,* eds. David W. Orme-Johnson, Lawrence H. Domash, and John T. Farrow. Los Angeles: MIU Press, 1974.

16. Reduced Use of Alcohol and Cigarettes
369–376. *Congressional Record,* Serial No. 92–1. Washington, D.C.: U.S. Government Printing Office, 1971.

17. Reduced Use of Nonprescribed Drugs
References: Robert Keith Wallace and Herbert Benson, "Decreased Drug Abuse with Transcendental Meditation: A Study of 1,862 Subjects," *Proceedings of the International*

Symposium on Drug Abuse, ed. C.J.A. Zarafonetis. Philadelphia: Lea and Febiger, 1972; 369–376. *Congressional Record,* Serial no. 92–1. Washington, D.C.: U.S. Government Printing Office, 1971.

18. Rehabilitation of Prisoners I
Reference: David W. Orme-Johnson, John Kiehlbauch, Richard Moore, and John Bristol, "Personality and Autonomic Changes in Meditating Prisoners." La Tuna Federal Penitentiary, New Mexico, 1972. To be submitted for publication.

19. Rehabilitation of Prisoners II
Reference: David W. Orme-Johnson, John Kiehlbauch, Richard Moore, and John Bristol, "Personality and Autonomic Changes in Meditating Prisoners." La Tuna Federal Penitentiary, New Mexico, 1972. To be submitted for publication.

20. Increased Self-Actualization
Reference: Philip C. Ferguson and John C. Gowan, "The Influence of Transcendental Meditation on Anxiety, Depression, Aggression, Neuroticism, and Self-Actualization." Paper presented at California State Psychological Association, Fresno, California, 1974.

21. Improved Mental Health
Reference: David W. Orme-Johnson, "Transcendental Meditation for Drug Abuse Counselors," *Scientific Research on Transcendental Meditation: Collected Papers Vol. 1,* eds. David W. Orme-Johnson, Lawrence H. Domash, and John T. Farrow. Los Angeles: MIU Press, 1974.

22. Improved Resistance to Disease I
Reference: Frank Papentin, "Self-Purification of the Organism and Transcendental Meditation: A Pilot Study," *Scientific Research on Transcendental Meditation: Collected Papers Vol. 1,* eds. David W. Orme-Johnson, Lawrence H. Domash, and John T. Farrow. Los Angeles: MIU Press, 1974.

23. Improved Resistance to Disease II
Frank Papentin, "Self-Purification of the Organism and

Transcendental Meditation: A Pilot Study," *Scientific Research on Transcendental Meditation: Collected Papers Vol. 1,* eds. David W. Orme-Johnson, Lawrence H. Domash, and John T. Farrow. Los Angeles: MIU Press, 1974.

24. Normalization of Weight

Reference: James T. Weldon and Arthur Aron, "Weight Change with Age and Transcendental Meditation," *Scientific Research on Transcendental Meditation: Collected Papers Vol. 1,* eds. David W. Orme-Johnson, Lawrence H. Domash, and John T. Farrow. Los Angeles: MIU Press, 1974.

25. Superior Perceptual-Motor Performance

Reference: Karen Blasdell, "The Effects of Transcendental Meditation upon a Complex Perceptual-Motor Task," *Scientific Research on Transcendental Meditation: Collected Papers Vol. 1,* eds. David W. Orme-Johnson, Lawrence H. Domash, and John T. Farrow. Los Angeles: MIU Press, 1974.

26. Faster Reaction Time

Reference: Robert Shaw and David Kolb, "One-Point Reaction Time Involving Meditators and Nonmeditators," *Scientific Research on Transcendental Meditation: Collected Papers Vol. 1,* eds. David W. Orme-Johnson, Lawrence H. Domash, and John T. Farrow. Los Angeles: MIU Press, 1974.

27. Improved Athletic Performance

Reference: M. Kesav Reddy, "The Effects of Transcendental Meditation on Athletic Performance." A.P. Sports Council, Lal Bahadur Stadium, Hyderabad, India.

28. Increased Normality

Reference: William P. Van den Berg and Bert Mulder, "Psychological Research on the Effects of Transcendental Meditation on a Number of Personality Variables Using the N.P.I.," *Scientific Research on Transcendental Meditation: Collected Papers Vol. 1,* eds. David W. Orme-Johnson, Lawrence H. Domash, and John T. Farrow. Los Angeles: MIU Press, 1974.

29. Increased Learning Ability

Reference: Allen I. Abrams, "Paired Associate Learning

and Recall: A Pilot Study Comparing Transcendental Meditators with Non-Meditators," *Scientific Research on Transcendental Meditation: Collected Papers Vol. 1*, eds. David W. Orme-Johnson, Lawrence H. Domash, and John T. Farrow. Los Angeles: MIU Press, 1974.

30. Increased Intelligence Growth Rate
    Reference: Andre S. Tjoa, "Some Evidence that the Practice of Transcendental Meditation Increases Intelligence as Measured by a Psychological Test," *Scientific Research on Transcendental Meditation: Collected Papers Vol. 1*, eds. David W. Orme-Johnson, Lawrence H. Domash, and John T. Farrow. Los Angeles: MIU Press, 1974.

31. Improved Academic Performance
    Second Reference (Study 2): Dennis P. Heaton and David W. Orme-Johnson, "Influence of Transcendental Meditation on Grade Point Average: Initial Findings," *Scientific Research on Transcendental Meditation: Collected Papers Vol. 1*, eds. David W. Orme-Johnson, Lawrence H. Domash, and John T. Farrow. Los Angeles: MIU Press. 1974.

32. Developed Personality
    First Reference: John Graham, "Auditory Discrimination in Meditators," *Scientific Research on Transcendental Meditation: Collected Papers Vol. I*, eds. David W. Orme-Johnson, Lawrence H. Domash, and John T. Farrow. Los Angeles: MIU Press, 1974.

33. Developed Intelligence
    Reference: David W. Orme-Johnson, "Psychological Testing of MIU Students: First Report," *Scientific Research on Transcendental Meditation: Collected Papers Vol. 1*, eds. David W. Orme-Johnson, Lawrence H. Domash, and John T. Farrow. Los Angeles: MIU Press, 1974.

34. *Āsanas*
    Reference: SIMS

BIBLIOGRAPHY

Aurobindo, Sri. *The Life Divine.* Pondicherry, India: India Library Society, 1965.

Aurobindo, Sri. *No Words—Acts.* Pondicherry, India: Ashram Trust Society, 1969.

Aurobindo, Sri. "Psychological Perfection," Compiled from the Mother's Talks. In *Sri Aurobindo Society Annual,* 1968.

Aurobindo, Sri. *The Teaching of Sri Aurobindo.* Pondicherry, India: Ashram Press.

Campbell, Anthony. *Seven States of Consciousness.* New York: Perennial Library, 1974.

Forem, Jack. *Transcendental Meditation.* New York: Dutton, 1973.

Gurdjieff, G.I. *Meetings with Remarkable Men.* New York: Dutton, 1963.

Hume, Robert Ernest. *The Thirteen Principle Upanishads.* New York: Oxford University Press, 1971.

Kenner, Hugh. *Bucky.* New York: William Morrow, 1973.

Krishnamurti, J. *Think on These Things.* New York: Perennial Library, 1964.

Krishnamurti, J. *Talks and Dialogues.* New York: Avon Books, 1968.

Merton, Thomas. *New Seeds of Contemplation.* New York: New Directions, 1972.

Ornstein, Robert. *The Psychology of Consciousness.* New York: The Viking Press, 1972.

Senzacki, Nyogen, and McCandless, Ruth S. *Buddhism and Zen.* New York: Philosophical Library, 1953.

Shah, Indries. *The Sufis.* Garden City: Doubleday, 1964.

Thoreau, Henry David. *Walden.* New York: Apollo Editions, 1966.
Yogi, Maharishi Mahesh. *Transcendental Meditation.* New York: Penguin, 1967.

PUBLISHED AND UNPUBLISHED PAPERS

American Foundation for Science of Creative Intelligence, "Creative Intelligence in Business." Los Angeles: Maharishi International University Press, 1972.

American Foundation for Science of Creative Intelligence, "Improving Performance and Productivity Through Stress Reduction." A Symposium for Management on TM and the Science of Creative Intelligence, Biltmore Hotel, New York, AFSCI National. Los Angeles: Maharishi International University Press, March 20, 1974.

Banquet, J.P. "Spectral Analysis of the EEG in Meditation." In *Electroencephalography and Clinical Neurophysiology.* Amsterdam: Elsevier Scientific Publishing Co., Vol 35., pp. 143–151, 1973.

Carrington, Patricia, and Ephron, Harmon S. "Meditation as an Adjunct to Psychotherapy." In *The World Biennial of Psychotherapy and Psychiatry,* edited by Silvano Arieti and Gerald Chrzanowski. New York: John Wiley and Sons, forthcoming.

Driscoll, Francis. "TM as a Secondary School Subject." In the *Phi Delta Kappan,* Vol. Liv. No. 4, p. 236. Los Angeles: December 1972.

Kanellakos, Demetri P., and Ferguson, Phillip C. "The Psychobiology of Transcendental Meditation." Maharishi International University Press, Spring 1973.

Levine, Paul H. "Transcendental Meditation and the Science of Creative Intelligence." In the *Phi Delta Kappan,* Vol. Liv. No. 4, p. 231. Los Angeles: December 1972.

Rubottom, Al E. "Transcendental Meditation and Its Potential Uses for Schools." In *Social Education,* pp. 851–857, December 1972.

Salerno, Robert L. "Brain-Mind Theories: A Conceptual Framework." In *Psychology 300,* March 31, 1974.

Shafi, Mohammed, Lavely, Richard and Jaffe, Robert. "Meditation and Marijuana." In *American Journal of Psychiatry,* Vol. 131, No. 1, pp. 60–63, January 1974.

Swinyard, Chester A., and Chaube, Shakuntala. "Neurological and Behavioral Aspects of Transcendental Meditation Relevant to Alcoholism: A Review." New York: *Annal of New York Academy of Sciences,* Vol. 233, pp. 162–173, 1974.

Sykes, David E. "Transcendental Meditation—as Applied to Criminal Justice Reform, Rehabilitation and Society in General." In *University of Maryland Law Forum,* Vol. III, No. 2, pp. 37–50, Winter 1973.

Wallace, Robert Keith, and Benson, Herbert. "The Physiology of Meditation." In *Alliance for Knowledge*. Los Angeles: Maharishi International University Press, 1973.

"Fundamentals of Progress." Maharishi International University Press, 1974.

INDEX

INDEX

Page references to charts are in *italic* typeface.